Changing Families
Changing Welfare

3/94

LIB/LEND/001

UNIVERSITY OF
WOLVERHAMPTON

Changing Families
Changing Welfare

Family Centres and the Welfare State

Crescy Cannan
University of Sussex

**HARVESTER
WHEATSHEAF**

New York   London   Toronto   Sydney   Tokyo   Singapore

First published 1992 by
Harvester Wheatsheaf
Campus 400, Maylands Avenue
Hemel Hempstead
Hertfordshire, HP2 7EZ
A division of
Simon & Schuster International Group

© 1992, Crescy Cannan

Typeset in 10/12pt Times
by Pentacor PLC

Printed in Great Britain by
BPCC Wheatons Ltd, Exeter

British Library Cataloguing in Publication Data

A catalogue record for this book is available from
the British Library

ISBN: 0 7450 1182 9 (hbk)
ISBN: 0 7450 1183 7 (pbk)

1 2 3 4 5   96 95 94 93 92

CONTENTS

PREFACE AND ACKNOWLEDGEMENTS

When I began this research in 1982, family centres were in an early stage of planning and development. By the time I finished, the 1989 Children Act had placed a duty on local authorities to establish a range of services, including family centres, to support families with children in need. The social practices – which family centres have exemplified – of working with families whose children were likely, through poverty or abuse, to enter local authority Care have been endorsed by the Children Act. The term 'in Care' formerly referred both to children in Care under court orders and to those in so-called 'voluntary' Care (also known as receptions into Care). Voluntary Care has now been abolished: since 1991, only those under court orders are 'in Care'; others are 'looked after' or receive services if they are in need. The Children Act represents, then, a shift to a lower boundary between families in need and local authority services: it stresses the sharing of responsibility and partnership with parents, and supporting rather than stigmatizing parents using support services.

These principles are at the heart of family centres; the Children Act has legitimized a form of social provision which has mushroomed since the 1970s and which, on close inspection, contains many of the conflicts inherent in social work and social welfare: care and control, stigma and compensation, professional power and user participation. Family centres – which, for the moment, we will define as social welfare centres for parents and children – tell us about a form of social provision ostensibly targeted on children in need and families under stress, but they also provide a case study in the broader functions, tensions and directions of social policy and social work in the 1990s. This book, then, is both an analysis and a historical account of family centres *per se*, and an examination of the politics of social welfare in the current restructuring of the welfare state. It is also a prescriptive book in that it attempts to draw on some of the creative work of family centres, and to give readers who work with children and families some pointers to good practice. This I define as that practice which opens opportunities to women and to children.

The research was based on observing ten family centres in the South of England and on the collection of documents from family centres, voluntary welfare organizations, local authorities' social services departments, and professional organizations. Altogether I collected material on 42 family centres in both statutory and voluntary sectors, in rural and urban areas, and in Conservative- and Labour-controlled councils. (The names of the family centres and their local authorities have been changed in the text.) I drew on the professional journals of the social work and child welfare professions, and the literature of political organizations, pressure groups, and voluntary child welfare organizations. My aims were to understand the processes and debates underlying what was seen in the social work profession as an exciting, innovative development. For comparison, I have observed and collected documents on a small number of French *centres socio-culturels*, so I shall be referring to French as well as British social and family policy.

This broad approach may risk obscuring detail in drawing overgeneralized conclusions. A major shortcoming, however, of micro-studies of the effectiveness of services is that they tend to ignore the wider impact of social practices as well as the constraints upon them. In my view it is the sociopolitical context and the ideological nature of family centres which must be understood if the significance of their rapid growth from the late 1970s is to be grasped. Family centres have emerged from debate and pressure-group activity: not surprisingly, they are diverse and often contradictory in practice. The resistance of ground-level professionals to certain aspects of policy, the different social welfare traditions to which they claimed loyalty, and the variety of ways in which the users are involved in centres have produced significant differences within this field of welfare.

A further advantage of breadth was that the sheer range of issues which social welfare addresses became apparent: my research has led me to examine developments in the fields of education, health care and delinquency as well as the general field of child and family welfare. This broad field of social provision has been understood as the context of which family centres are an expression, and it is this broader context that enables me to examine how family centres are part of a system that regulates parenthood, and especially motherhood. Of great concern are the low level and uneven quality of provision for children: family centres are indicative of the low priority of children in general in the UK, for, as I shall go on to argue, they represent an attempt to push informal care back on to families rather than to expand public services to children. Family centres, then, provide a case study in the way in which social welfare, children's rights and gender roles are interwoven at a time when the boundary between family and state is being renegotiated.

Acknowledgements

While the responsibility for this book remains my own, there are many people who have provided me with material and helped me to think through the issues. I would like to thank all the people I interviewed in family centres; many wondered whether this was yet another piece of research which would take up their time but would never see the light of day. This book is a repayment for their time and ideas. I cannot name all of the people who helped, but will single out Jan Phelan and Chris Warren for letting me see their research on family centres, and for their help with contacts. Gerry Stimson supervised the orginal research at Goldsmiths' College, London University, and, like Marion Lowe, who read a near-final draft, provided me with detailed and perceptive feedback. Didier le Gall at the University of Caen and Monsieur LeMasson of the Caen Caisse d'Allocations Familiales set up my French visits and explained much about French social provision to me. The Lady Allen of Hurtwood Trust helped with the expenses of that part of the fieldwork. I must thank my colleagues and friends in the School of Cultural and Community Studies at the University of Sussex, especially Hugh England, Stuart Laing, Barry Luckock and Nick Tucker, each of whom has, in different ways, provided me with the support and stimulation that have underpinned the production of this book. And finally I would like to thank my mother, Joan Cannan, for her help in looking after my son: without that help the book would not indeed have seen the light of day.

CHAPTER 1

THE FAMILY AND THE STATE

Introduction

This book is a case study of the shifting boundary between family and state in Britain. It will look at the growth of family centres from the mid 1970s onwards in order to describe the processes by which private family responsibilities and public state responsibilities have been realigned and underlined. While this shifting boundary became especially visible during the Conservative (New Right) restructuring of state welfare in the 1980s, I shall show that there is a long British tradition of maintaining a high boundary between the family and the state: state reluctance to share the care of children or other dependent people with their families is not something novel but, rather, is consistent with British attitudes to the family as a domain quite separate from the public. What we see is a case of family and 'community' responsibilities being stated more forcibly at a time when local government was being deprived of its powers and resources by a strong central government, which simultaneously promoted the expansion of the voluntary (not-for-profit) and the private (commercial) sectors in social care. I shall be looking, then, *not* just at New Right social policies but also at Labour Party and Social Democratic policies, at the role and attitudes of the social-work profession, at the voluntary childcare organizations, and at local authority social services departments in the period 1972 to 1990.

If it can be shown that social provision is the outcome of a political struggle (rather than simply the imposition of dominant ideas), what are the implications for the services themselves: whose needs do they serve, what characterizes their users? I shall consider the deeper implications of family centres, asking whether – given that they grow from the demise of daycare and residential care for children – they support women in their care of their children, and whether they can promote opportunities or a more just allocation of domestic tasks. I shall also be concerned for children: are family centres an effective way of promoting healthy childhood, and how do they compare with childcare provision in other European countries? To anticipate a little: I shall show that, while we can find examples of good practice, as a *system* family centres are highly unstable: they are diverse, variable in coverage, aims, and above all in quality. I shall return to issues of accountability, equity, equal opportunities, and quality in the final chapter.

Chapter 2 will survey the range of types of family centres, Chapters 3 and 4 will examine their roots in discourses on child welfare and the 'crisis' in the family. Chapter 5 will consider the role of social work in family centres, and Chapter 6 will attempt to prescribe a theoretical and practical framework for good practice. In this chapter I shall set out the social context of family centres, and raise the gender issues which will pervade the book. I shall argue that family centres have obscured these, despite the fact that most of their users are women (89 per cent in Warren's [1990] national survey), and that existing research into and accounts of family centres produced within the social-work profession tell us only part of the story.

British social policy is based on a tradition of family privacy: rather than the state sharing in the tasks of rearing future citizens and supporting families by reducing the strain on carers (women), there is a dominant view that 'normal' families would not want or need state intervention which should, rather, be reserved for the feckless, deviant or inadequate (Finch, 1989; Riley, 1983). Part of the regulatory quality of family centres lies in their connection of maternal behaviour, family life and child abuse. Alternative discourses on child welfare problems have been marginalized – especially the demand for universal, public daycare for children. There is a long history of using child abuse as an issue to define 'normal' families and their domestic roles and responsiblities

(Frost and Stein, 1989; Gordon, 1988; Parton, 1985); in this perspective only abusive or 'problem' families 'need' services; the majority cope, and therefore do not need them.

Family centres have diverse philosophical roots: while they regulate in ways we shall explore, they also have the potential to provide welfare services which mesh with users' stated needs and promote opportunities. It is my view that in the 1990s professions and the welfare state, far from being intrusive of or damaging to working-class life (as was argued by left libertarians such as Geach and Szwed [1983]), actually neglect need, especially the needs of those groups who are unattractive or socially under-valued: the alcoholics, the elderly mentally ill, the chronically mentally ill, lone mothers, abused women, depressed women – all these receive too little material and social assistance from the welfare state (Brown and Harris, 1978; Dingwall *et al.*, 1983; Edwards, 1989; Illsey, 1981; Scull, 1984; Sedgwick, 1982). Women are forced back into traditional caring roles – through lack of alternatives and through lack of assistance in their tasks. In the field of care of disabled and elderly people this is starkly evident: an ideology of caring as 'natural' for women has legitimated the placing of community care in the family. Reviewing the now extensive research on the impact for carers, Dalley (1988) says:

> The experiences recounted in study after study revealthcrealityofcommunitycarepoliciesforbothcarerandcared for alike. There is pervasive lack of choice ... the professional services – hostels, group homes, home nursing, home helps, day care, respite care – which are envisaged by service providers as comprising community care, are every-where proving insufficient, even where bolstered by volun-tary organization support. The networks of neighbours, friends and extended kin may *help* on a sporadic and irregular basis ... but rarely match the expectations defined as care *by* the community. Most often, care-giving devolves on to those closest to the dependent person – and those deemed to be closest are generally wives, mothers and daughters – or the dependent person is left to cope alone. (Dalley, 1988: 7)

Women and children need services and support from the state, and it seems to me that it is mistaken to dismiss state welfare as damaging to working-class families. Violence to children or women should be publicly responded to with protection and support for victims and control and treatment of perpetrators. In caring for children, just as for other dependent people, women should receive support and validation in the form of a range of daycare and respite services, and they should be able to choose the form of service that suits their needs. Lack of social provision is counter to children's needs for sociability and stimulation, and counter to women's rights to work or train or engage in public life. This book, then, is concerned with the quality of service provided to families as a whole *and* to women and children in their own right, and it will ask how much the discourses on the 'crisis' in the family and on welfare dependence have legitimated a decline in *services* for families.

Family centres: from welfare dependence to parental responsibility

Family centres began to appear in the mid 1970s, with rapid growth from the early 1980s, totalling around 500 centres nationally by the late 1980s (Warren, 1990). They have been greeted by social workers and childcare organizations as a positive development, something innovative and progressive. Their manifest aims have been to promote the care of children in their own families, to prevent children coming into public Care, and to support families in need. Before the 1989 Children Act children could be taken into Care on a court order (compulsory Care), or by parents' consent (voluntary Care). But so-called voluntary Care could harden into a long-term form of Care with parents losing their rights, and the system was heavily stigmatized (see Chapter 3 for a full account of the critiques of the Care system). By the mid 1970s there was concern at these processes, and the prevention of receptions into Care became a goal of social services departments. Family centres were established to work with families on the brink of the Care system, and they will continue the same role under the Children Act. The term 'in Care' under the Children Act refers to those under court orders; others will be 'in need' or using support services such as family centres to prevent the need for compulsory court procedures, and to promote the care of children by their own families.

Family centres are targeted on areas of social deprivation and seen as 'preventive' resources: preventing entry into Care, child abuse, isolation and loneliness in mothers. They are run by statutory social services departments, voluntary organizations, or sometimes by consortia or partnerships of self-help, voluntary and statutory organizations. Some have a clear social work role, others a more open, neighbourhood approach. Despite the optimism associated with them, however, there is some concern in the family centre world as to their aims (are they too broad, how do we know what is effective?) (Gibbons, 1990; The Short Report, 1984). It is this underlying concern with latent as well as manifest aims which I shall be concerned to unravel.

That the clientele of family centres are both worked on and receive a service is characteristic of service organizations (Blau and Scott, 1963); associated with this is strong professional power in negotiating the nature of clients' problems and the manner of their solution. However, the 'character work' (Strong, 1979), the behavioural focus, of some family centres reveals something else: these centres are not just providing a service to their users, they are also what Blau and Scott refer to as 'commonweal organiza-tions' – set up for the public at large, so that by containing and treating deviant families, they benefit society. All family centres convey norms of socialization and parenthood, but they convey them directly and individually in their social work and collectively through the participation of conforming local people where there is more of a community work orientation.

In this time of welfare reconstruction, family centres serve another commonweal function: that of disseminating norms of welfare consumption and an ideal of family independence. In many centres the goal of preventing welfare dependence, of checking consumption of day and residential childcare services (and of rehabilitating from such dependence), has been as important an aim as that of child protection and prevention of entry into Care (Cannan, 1990). Oaklands Family Centre provides an example of this aim. The social services managers and the project organizer had to produce a plan acceptable to a Conservative county council committed to limiting expenditure and encouraging informal care and self-responsibility. The centre's aims (as set out in its literature) were:

to help reduce the need for families with financial, domestic and child related problems becoming dependent clients of statutory welfare agencies.

Another centre aimed:

wherever possible to allow parents and children to become-less dependent on the Centre through reduction of attendance.

One director of social services introduced his department's strategy in 1984 as:

a major shift in emphasis towards an effective preventive strategy . . . . It is my firm belief that the recommendations contained in this report will ensure that [the] department remains in the forefront of national developments.

His department's new policy was to replace residential childcare provision with locally based services, which aimed to support children at home rather than removing them: 'risks may need to be taken in order to avoid the well-recognised consequences of care'.

During the 1970s and 1980s both residential care and day nurseries were portrayed in local authority strategy documents (such as those quoted from above) as causing problems because of the separation of parent (mother) and child, as being emotionally unhealthy environments, and as encouraging irresponsibility in parents. An assumption was made that future 'dependence' on social services would be prevented by diverting clients from them, using therapeutic and community development methods to achieve this. Reducing dependence and promoting responsibility are, therefore, aims in most social services family centres, and indeed of the voluntary centres, for they are part of the 'community', and usually part-funded by local authorities' social services departments to increase informal community resources. Not only do most of these centres aim to reduce dependence on the statutory agencies, but they talk of changing parents' behaviour and providing 'the minimum services necessary to enable a family to cope', and measuring 'success against those families able to move on or at least, reduce their hours of attendance'.

This aim must be seen in the context of financial pressures on local authorities: during the 1970s and 1980s childcare projects were typically funded by the central government Urban Programme or by local authority grants. A series of government Initiatives provided short-term central funding through consortia of voluntary agencies' projects within Department of Health and Social Security (DHSS) criteria. The most significant initiatives for family centres were the Under Fives Initiative of £6m over three years from 1983, which helped 45 local projects (Holman, 1986), and Opportunities for Volunteers, with £5.5m over three years from 1982. The minute scale of this funding is clear when it is compared to a typical social services department annual budget of £15m at that time (which was still insufficient to meet demand). The majority of family centre documents, whether from Conservative- or traditional Labour-controlled areas, colluded with this situation of underfunding by portraying dependence on services as an 'obvious' problem. 'Prevention' meant restricting use of child welfare services, for the conventional wisdom was that 'Care' was a bad (and expensive) thing, and that use of social-work services could start a Care career.

The social workers and other family centre workers in my study tended to view being in Care negatively, and used labelling theory to refer to the danger of developing deviant careers, especially in the senses of mental illnesses, criminality, or poor future parenting. Packman (1981) also noted this in her research on social work practice with children. This attitude partly arose from the concern expressed from the 1970s onwards that too many children were in Care. Under the Labour government this concern was officially voiced in the Short Report of 1984 on *Children in Care*. These children were overwhelmingly from poor families, and it was argued that social services departments should strive to support such families rather than splitting them up (Holman, 1976). While noting the shortage of daycare and that easier access to daycare would help families at risk of losing their children into Care, the Short Report did not recommend an increase in daycare; rather, it advocated more childminding for under-2s as a welcome, 'less institutional' approach (paras 44–5).

At the same time, radical social and community workers were taking up the issues of parents' rights, arguing that professionals abused their power in work with 'problem families' and demanding instead solidarity with and participation by the poor (Liffman, 1978; Thomas, 1983). This movement was contemporary with the legal rights movement (among prisoners, claimants, and psychiatric patients) which, in this context, produced the Family Rights Group in 1975, which continues to campaign for and argue for adequate legal representation of families involved in Care proceedings (Tunnard, 1987).

While these movements stressed the rights of the poor and of natural parents, some of the impetus for family centres came from those who voiced different criticisms of social workers, arguing for more decisive practice and planning (e.g. Goldstein, *et al.*, 1973). The fostering and adoption lobby argued that once in Care children tended to drift aimlessly downwards, and that such children could be released for permanent fostering or adoption (Rowe and Lambert, 1973). From all sides there was criticism of childcare services, a marginalization of the campaigns such as the National Child Care Campaign, which called for expanded and improved daycare services for children. 'Prevention' meant (as it had meant since the 1948 Children Act) keeping children out of institutional services rather than improving the range and quality of those services.

The 1970s, then, brought critiques of state welfare from Right and Left: social workers were described as patronizing and as mystifying social or personal problems (the Left view), or mollycoddling those who would otherwise learn independence (the Right view). Responsibility and independence became a theme – and not just in the social sphere: in the health field, initial optimism on the establishment of the National Health Service was checked by rising costs, especially of hospital care and treatment, and by rising demand. DHSS documents such as *Prevention and Health – Everybody's business* (1976) stressed that individuals must modify their own behaviour to improve their health. Graham (1979), commenting on these documents, shows how the path to good health was seen to lie in health education and the assumption of personal responsibility for healthy lifestyles. Further, in the case of children's health, maternal responsibility in meeting children's needs – emotional, intellectual and physical – was the keystone. Thus, in medicine, prevention became identified with health education and the promotion of healthy lifestyles within the physical and emotional life of the family (Davies, 1984).

Strong views on parental responsibility were expressed by the Magistrates' Association (Tutt, 1981), which urged the Conservative government to revert to more custodial regimes for delinquents. The 1980 White Paper on *Young Offenders* stated:

> the Government believes it is important that the courts should . . . be able more effectively to bring home to parents their responsibilities in relation to juveniles who offend. . . .
> (Home Office, 1980: para. 53)

This stress on parental responsibility for crimes of children under 16 and the aim of making parents accountable for their children's actions were incorporated in the 1982 Criminal Justice Act, with a stronger version proposed in the 1990 White Paper on *Crime, Justice and Protecting the Public*. In the event, the issue has proved contentious. While Conservative Party conferences have applauded the aim of *making* parents responsible, concerted opposition from magistrates and organizations such as the Children's Legal Centre and NACRO (the National Association for the Care and Resettlement of Offenders) has prevented this becoming a reality because of the impossibility (and questionable effectiveness) of implementing it amongst families who may be too poor or incapable of enforcing discipline over their children (Hoghughi, 1991; *The Magistrate*, July 1991).

The 1989 Children Act, like the White Papers on criminal justice and on child maintenance (*Children Come First* [DSS, 1990], which preceded the Child Support Act 1991), places a strong emphasis on parental responsibility. Lord Mackay, the Lord Chancellor, stated that it was the 'golden thread' that ran through the Act, and that:

> The Government is anxious . . . to make it clear in the Bill that families should generally be left to sort out matters for themselves unless it is shown that without an order the child's welfare will suffer. (Mackay, 1989: 505).

The Act is a minimalist piece of legislation; its chief aims are twofold: first to diminish the need for children to come into Care, and second to promote the care and upbringing of children within their families by providing support for families in need. That is to say, it places a general duty on local authorities to safeguard and promote the welfare of chidren in their areas who are in need, *and* to promote the upbringing of such children by their own families. The state should intervene only where families fail; it has no general duty to all children or families.

Such is the legislative and policy context of British family centres. For this research some comparisons have been made with French *centres socio-culturels*, and their social policy context. The most striking difference is that the French see *use* of services as expressive of good citizenship and supportive of family life in general. The state's responsibility to ensure a high level of social protection is not debated. The family is seen not as separate from the state, but as part of a continuum of social institutions which link individual to society. Hence, as Ely and Stanley (1990) puts it:

> the French do not see the interests of the individual, the family, the local community and the state as necessarily separate or opposed to the degree that we do. French people certainly believe in advancing themselves through their own efforts. But the ideal of the self-sufficient family is foreign to their way of thinking, and if they become aware of it, they tend to associate it only with the very rich. Their habitual mode of thinking is to claim that each citizen has a number of natural rights which all other citizens, society and state should sustain. The list of rights asserted varies with the argument being made, but personnel in this field [of child welfare] begin enumerating the rights of children with the right to be cared for – which infers a claim on the family, local community, society and the state services . . . .Our own political and legal philosophy has shown greater develop-ment in the direction of limiting the power of the state over the individual, stressing an opposition between their inter-ests, giving us a different conception of rights. (Ely and Stanley, 1990: 3–4)

French social policy as developed during the 1980s emphasizes the task of reintegration [*insertion*], of bringing groups together rather than allowing a splitting apart of society. With rising poverty and unemployment, especially among youth, and limits to economic growth, the French socialist government of 1981–6 challenged social workers, youth workers, the police, those in the fields of sport and leisure, and local politicians to work together to find ways of meeting social needs and preventing crime, delin-quency and exclusion (King, 1988). The Ninth Plan of 1984–8 emphasized social development of neighbourhoods and action aimed at groups rather than individuals – for instance in measures in favour of immigrants, and the social integration of

young people. The Ninth Pl[...]
increase in daycare services a[...]
parents' needs (Leprince, 1991: 24)[...]
been met, there has been considerabl[...]
the initiatives of *Caisse Nationale d'Alloca*[...]
– the principal family benefits fund – and t[...]
French municipalities and communes to i[...]
facilities. Decentralization of government has pro[...]
local administrations who have an interest in the eff[...]
these programmes in their areas (Garrish, 1986; Meny, [...]
contrast with the situation in the UK, where decentralizatio[...]
been associated with a reduction in the powers of lo[...]
government (Glennester *et al.*, 1991).

Social work is involved in the search for new forms of social
protection, which integrate rather than exclude – validating
users by integrating them in social groups, in employment, or into
using universal services, rather than marginalizing them as clients
with separate stigmatizing services (Collins, 1990; Thévenet and
Désigaux, 1985). The CNAF, whose centres will be described in
Chapter 6, has rethought its policies and provision in the light of
the 'crisis' of the welfare state: its experience during the 1970s
and 1980s was of rising demand for benefits and growing numbers
of 'new' poor on long-term benefits – especially amongst lone
parents. Allying itself firmly with government thinking on the
importance of maintaining social solidarity by developing neighbourhoods and reaching *les précaires* (those in precarious circumstances), and in accordance with its aim of supporting families
and improving services for children, it announced in 1987 that
social action would henceforth be part of its means of supporting
the family, and that social work would be one method of
developing this mission (CNAF 1987–8). The social action wing of
CNAF complements the family benefits wing, the two adding up to
a policy of supporting the family through *both* universalist and
targeted provision, through material and social-work help.

Natalist attitudes on both right and left wings in France have
resulted in generous child and family benefits designed to remove
parents' difficulties in rearing children, and to encourage them to
perform their tasks well. Daycare is also considered to be good
for children: a socializing and stimulating force which benefits the
community. France provides nearly 107,000 day nursery places

also included in its priorities an
their better adaptation to
Though the targets have not
expansion, partly due to
ons Familiales (CNAF)
incentives given to
crease childcare
ced powerful
tiveness of
987) – a
has
cal

|uarter of that
nursery school,
prince, 1991).
school holidays
ents are neither
altes-garderies –
to twenty hours
ing mothers, and
thers. There are
d holiday centres
ople. The *centres*
n sociale provide a
d young people,
t chapters I will
s we can learn for

Family policy: the support and regulation of mothers

In the 1980s and 1990s 'social control' is too blunt a concept for analyzing the relationship between welfare organizations and their users (and potential users); 'social regulation' more accurately describes the often non-coercive, always ideological character of social welfare (Donzelot, 1980), and takes into account the diversity of professions and welfare organizations and their struggle in the changing welfare marketplace. I shall argue that regulation occurs directly through the *kinds* of services and supervision seen in family centres, and through the way these regulate *images* of the responsible and independent family. Family centres are part of familist social policies, which stress the naturalness of caring within the family by women rather than the desirability of shared care by the collectivity, in the public domain (Dalley, 1988).

Regulation may be through ideological, economic or legal means. The taxation and social security systems underpin the roles and duties of husband and wife (Land, 1979, 1989; Lewis, 1989; McIntosh, 1978, 1984). The laws on marriage and divorce are means by which the state regulates marriage, but more fundamentally, 'in supporting marriage the state supports a particular exploitative relationship between men and women' (Barker, 1978: 239). Marriage, then, is regulated and adapted so that its participants will continue to perform their functions of socialization and social reproduction; but marriage and the family are unlike more public institutions such as education, the community, industry, the media. The family, according to the principles of British liberalism, is private, and that privacy is taken to be the bastion which protects the individual from the encroachments of the state (Mount, 1982). The boundaries between state and family are constantly challenged: conservatives (I refer to traditional attitudes rather than to political parties) see too much intervention in the family as weakening it, yet child abuse and neglect demand intervention as children are a national asset requiring public health and education services while remaining the responsibility of the private family. This dilemma is central to the functioning of family centres.

Barker (1978) shows how legal and moral views of marriage have adapted to the shift from 'natural' family unit to the individualism which is characterized by a contractual relationship. The Anglican Church, for example, tends now to hold a 'romantic' view of marriage: to see it as a freely chosen relationship in which there should be interference only when things go seriously wrong. Barker uses the term 'repressive benevolence' to describe this form of regulation, which provides a measure of protection and legal rights to women and children, while at the same time upholding the institution as a whole, with its advantages for men. Morgan (1985) sees this as a shift from viewing marriage as an institution to a twentieth-century view of marriage as a relationship: less a cluster of roles than a source of personal growth and well-being. In his study of the Home Office/ DHSS report *Marriage Matters* (1979) he shows how the authors put forward a 'modern' idea of marriage as increasingly companionate and egalitarian, with divorce and separation as acceptable as long as they occur only in a minority of cases. Marital problems are equated not with structural causes but with interpersonal distress and disharmony. Counselling, 'caring professions' and 'caring agencies' (which were well represented on the committee) are put forward as self-evidently a good thing. Morgan argues that marital problems are both treated and constructed by medical, psychoanalytic and counselling professions: regulation consists partly in this construction – in what Donzelot calls the 'regulation of images' (1980: 169 ff). Morgan also rests his views on Foucault's: systems of ideas themselves discipline; by classifying and interpreting couples' legitimate and illegitimate sexual pleasures, the professions simultaneously manage them. Since Morgan's and Donzelot's work was published, family therapy has become a major technology of social-work intervention into family life; accordingly, in Chapter 5 I shall examine its assumptions, possibilities and limitations.

Donzelot's work is an examination of modern non-coercive means of regulating family life which have developed over the last century. He sees the state regulating family life in order to check the dangerous forces of individualism and working-class solidarity: the dependent wife and child are a means of instilling labour discipline in men. The mother is cultivated by the professions of medicine, education and social work as their auxiliary, normalizing and moralizing working-class families with 'modern' bourgeois practices. However, the new education and child-rearing practices which gave bourgeois children 'protected liberation' offer only a form of 'supervised freedom' and surveillance to the working-class child. While previously the family was ordered through the delegation of state powers to the father, now the family is the object and creation of the state, and a means of regulating the relationship between individual and society. Health, education and welfare services compose this system of regulation; conforming families retain their privacy and autonomy according to liberal principles, whereas non-conforming families risk falling into supervision by state professionals: the mother becomes both ally and target of professionals. Child abuse provides a legitimate ground for intervention in working-class family life, while simultaneously providing a means of promoting, through social work, the ideal 'normal' family (Gordon, 1988).

Family centres take middle-class norms – not just of traditional roles and authority, but of creativity and personal growth – to areas of social need. The middle classes increasingly turn to counsellors or therapists for guidance or to ease distress, but their experience may be different from that of the working-class woman who is receiving a psychotherapeutic service from a social

worker: the one may liberate
(despite espousing liberationist
growth) be focused on gender
competence rather than on insig
reasons for this lie not in the soci
kind of service within which she or
set up for disadvantaged families,
satory education, 'it follows ... that
for the something which is lacking in
(Bernstein, 1971: 192).

Sociologists of crime and deviance
layered regulation of women – welfa   ...orced
by informal controls such as gossip   ...aming) – when
discussing why women commit fewer crimes than men (Heidensohn, 1985). Women experience a greater variety of means of
control than do men, and the variety of sanctions include
judgements on women's esteem and mothering through social
work and psychiatry. It has been shown that women criminals are
judged as double failures: as criminals and as inadequate women.
Edwards (1984, 1989) shows how women – as criminals and as
victims – are more likely to be processed in terms of their gender
role, and punished for deviance from the feminine. Women are
therefore more prone, like juveniles, to be processed through
the welfare system rather than the criminal justice system.
Family centres, like social work and psychiatry, must be seen as
part of that system of social regulation, part of a continuum of
control of gender-role behaviour from the informal to the formal
and punitive.

Part of the explanation for this tension lies in the mother's role
as agent of social reproduction: ideally, the mother should be
able to socialize her child so as to create a person who can
integrate him/herself into the school system, and take his/her
place in the labour market. Working-class mothers, and certainly
those in deprivation or alone, may not always have adequate
personal or material resources to achieve this unless they are
aided by the social welfare system. This is a particularly acute
problem for lone mothers, and for mothers in deprived areas
which lack the resources and social infrastructure of more middle-
class areas. Family centres are a new form of support to poor
families, but they have sprung out of the demise of public day
nurseries and children's homes, which formerly aided them.

s based on a fundamentally different attitude
ch: it asserts that children are a private indulgence
rather than future citizens requiring direct state
ent (Baker, 1986). There appears to be a fear in the
sh mind that too much in the way of public childcare and
amily support services will somehow encourage fecklessness, an abdication from responsibilities. While the post-war settlement included a welfare state of universal services in the fields of health care and education, this was not the case in pre-school provision. It has been well documented (e.g. Riley, 1983) that the extensive system of wartime day nurseries was reframed as damaging children's mental health through maternal deprivation: public daycare for working-class families in Britain has become associated with problem families – an issue which will be the concern of the final chapter.

The Conservative administrations of the 1980s have preferred to promote private nurseries, and partnerships of employers, parents' groups and voluntary agencies for those who want daycare for children. For those who cannot pay, Conservative 'pro-family' policies have worsened their position. As Becker and Golding (1991) have shown:

> In 1987, just over 5.5 million people in families with children lived on incomes below 50% of the average . . . . Families with children have been particularly hard hit. From 1979 to 1987 the proportion of all children living in families whose income was 50% below average income more than doubled, from 12% to 26%, this was three million children in 1987.
> (Becker and Golding, 1991: 15)

Women have been particularly hard hit in this feminization of poverty, both through low wages and precarious employment and because so many lone mothers are dependent on benefit. The Conservative government's attempt to break dependency on the state and increase family responsibilities has had a paradoxical effect. Craig and Glendinning (1990) interviewed twenty families in touch with childcare and community-work services, three-quarters of whom were lone parents, all of whom were on benefit:

> these families had no alternative but to depend on others to make ends meet. Parents, boyfriends, boyfriends' families

and even their own adult children all helped out. (Craig and
Glendinning, 1990: 24)

The decline in the level of their state benefits made these
families feel more vulnerable, for the shift to dependence on
families was humiliating, but it was also damaging to relationships
within families. The attempt to break the culture of dependence
on the state had actually undermined the family: what might have
been supportive relationships (in responsible families) were
tested to their limits, paradoxically forcing women back on to the
state.

Issues in welfare pluralism

It will be evident, when we come to look at examples of family
centres and to explain their origins, that 'welfare pluralism' – a
strategy for realigning the relationship between the state and its
public – has a central place. The welfare state is generally taken
to have four sectors: the statutory, the voluntary (or not-for-profit),
the informal, and the private or commercial. In the early 1970s
the New Right and sections of the Left had decried state welfare
as destructive of 'natural' communities and families on the one
hand, and as unnecessarily controlling and intrusive in working-
class life on the other. The oil crisis in 1973–4 was used to
legitimate retrenchment in state expenditure on public services.
In all 'advanced' capitalist countries the balance of welfare
provision was being reconsidered, and social work's role was
changing: social care resources were now to be found in the
community itself, in informal networks, self-help groups, in
families: all areas where women would be affected as producers
as well as consumers of social and health care.

The voluntary sector has had to tread a delicate path in this
context. It has been eager to rise to the invitation to play a larger
part in the welfare state – a part greatly reduced by the post-war
establishment of state welfare, and by the establishment of large
social services departments in 1971. But it has been emphatic that
it should not substitute for statutory services, or seek to promote
its own growth at the expense of state provision. (The voluntary
sector, however, is diverse – not all organizations have shared

this view.) Yet it has participated in debates on the supposed 'crisis in the family' – debates which have, as we shall see, produced policies which have reiterated traditional gender roles in the community and in the family. Family centres illustrate the shifting balance in the sectors of the welfare state: both voluntary and informal sectors have had their responsibilities increased at a time when the statutory services have pulled back from broad principles of prevention and universalism to targeted 'heavy-end' intervention.

The effect of the post-war welfare state was to cast the voluntary organizations – which had their origins in the late nineteenth century – into a subordinate, residual role. The family and child welfare organizations responded by becoming more specialist – for instance, running homes for handicapped children, or adoption services, or children's homes in which local authorities could place children in Care; they saw their role as complementing the state system with a specialist, professional organization. At the same time they have argued that they promote humanitarian values, and opportunities for voluntary service, and that they bridge the gap between electors and elected by encouraging participation in the formal system.

The voluntary organizations have characterized themselves as a voluntary *movement*. Lord Wolfenden's Report in 1978 stressed both the moral contribution of the voluntary sector (through opportunities for participation) and the possibility of more pluralism in the British welfare state. The Report was eagerly seized upon by the Conservative government. The Conservatives were repeatedly to state their support for the voluntary sector:

> I believe that the volunteer movement is at the heart of all our social welfare provision. That the statutory services are the supportive ones underpinning, where necessary filling the gaps and helping the helpers. (Margaret Thatcher to the WRVS in 1981, quoted in Brenton, 1985: 177).
>
> . . . it must be recognized that there are limits to what the state can and *should* do in meeting the needs of the community . . . . Just as much as self-reliance and self-confidence are the keys to personal success, so self-help and mutual assistanceare the foundations of family, neighbourhood and com-munity life. (Timothy Raison, speech to the Volunteer Movement in 1980, quoted in *ibid.*: 178)

Simultaneously the nascent Social Democratic Party (SDP) raised the question of a more mixed economy of welfare. Their top–down approach argued that if services were decentralized, and if there were more public participation, then services would be more efficient and responsive to need. The caring networks and groups in the community should be supported and encouraged by social workers rather than being duplicated by state services. Hatch and Hadley (1981) recast the state as enabler, regulator of service providers in a mixed system. In this they echo the Barclay Report's (1982) call for community social work, and the earlier Seebohm Report (1968) (the forerunner of the social services departments). Hatch and Hadley's book is explicitly linked with the SDP, but it was enthusiastically endorsed by Michael Meacher of the Labour Party and Sir George Young of the Conservative Party. Hadley was influential in the welfare 'establishment' and, as an advocate of decentralized social services, was a consultant to one of the social services departments in this study which, in its planning documents, described a new family centre's objective to be:

> To continually seek to achieve a situation whereby the family is enabled to care supported by the facilities in their natural community. It must be recognized that in an ideal situation problems with the family would be met by support from the natural community. . . .

In similar vein, three Swindon family centres workers agreed that:

> Family projects have highlighted the fact that giving structure and legitimacy to the natural caring forces in a community and support for their development is a vitally important area for social work, health and education to consider. . . . Family projects are initially about developing initiative and preventive work which will complement the work of the local authority Social Services Department. This work . . . also aims to develop the latent strengths and resources in the areas by working with rather than for the people who live there . . . . (Thamesdown Voluntary Service Centre, n.d. : 11)

Beresford and Croft (1984) argued that the Conservative government under Margaret Thatcher did not appear to need the legitimation of welfare pluralists or voluntary organizations. Rather, we see Fabianism moving to the right, accommodating itself to the dominant discourse on welfare pluralism. In so doing, the welfare pluralists have fudged practical issues of funding (especially the difference between volunteer and voluntary services) and ideological issues on the role of women as carers, despite the evidence that community care is exploitative of women's labour. Decentralization was also an aim of the new municipal socialism of the 1980s (Croft and Beresford, 1989; Frost and Stein, 1989); again, the approach is essentially top–down: more citizen access and involvement, but no real growth in service democratization.

While women predominate in voluntary organizations (as both users and providers of formal and informal care), the question of gender is obscured and sidestepped. The proponents of pluralism also gloss over the fact that many voluntary organizations have become like statutory organizations in the professionalization of their workforces. Nor do they examine by what means participation and accountability will become a reality. Instead of analysis, we find rhetoric: local, informal, voluntary, community and neighbourhood are contrasted with state, formal, bureaucratic, professional, centralized. The voluntary organizations, then, were and are faced with a dilemma: they are keen to promote their ideals of service and participation, yet they tend to be committed to a belief in *state* welfare which they would complement. While they would like to develop more participative models of social welfare, they may not wish this to replace statutory provision or to increase the burden on the informal sectors (Johnson, 1987).

Most of the big voluntary childcare organizations appointed social policy advisers in the early 1970s to help negotiate a place in and policy on the changing welfare state. One adviser explained that there was no set policy in her organization, so that as a result the field workers set the pace on community development. Their approach meshed with the organization principle that the projects should be responsible to local people and should reflect their definitions of need. At the same time she was concerned lest local action and volunteering were exploited by government attempts to find cheap alternatives to statutory services. Family centres provide an example of how these dilemmas are played out in practice, and how a shift in the balance between statutory, informal and voluntary sectors comes about.

Issues for the 1990s

In most EC countries the family is presumed to need an infrastructure of public or semi-public services – daycare and leisure services for children and youth, health care to which entitlement should be widened rather than restricted, training and programmes to promote equal opportunities for women, improved parental leave and employment protection schemes. In most Northern European countries there is a sense that society forms an organic entity, and that the state has a social responsibility to the individual citizen as well as to society as a whole. The British Conservative government's refusal to endorse the EC 'Social Charter' in 1989 and its opt-out of the social chapter of the Treaty on European Economic and Political Union in 1991 reveal the adherence of the British New Right to North American individualism rather than progressive European thinking.

So rather than the responsible state, the British government has promoted the responsible family which should provide for itself, maintaining a distance from the state. The state should provide minimal services for those in extreme need or those who are a danger to society. Lone parents have become a target group: not so much a group in need as the carriers and creators of social problems. Margaret Thatcher, in a lecture to the National Children's Home in 1990, reiterated her view on the apparent crisis in parental responsibility:

> 'children are in danger of seeing life without fathers not as the exception but as the rule and recently, I read of a school attended by so many children of single mothers that one child whose father had come to see the school play was so embarrassed at being different that she asked him not to come to her school any more. This is a new kind of threat to our whole way of life, the long term implications of which we can hardly grasp.'

Conservative family policy has attempted to force families back to traditional roles – as witnessed by the new policies for child maintenance (DSS, 1990), in which 'errant fathers' are to be made more responsible (and the state less) for payments to their children. Coote *et al.* (1990), in seeking to develop a Labour Party response to this and a policy which moves on from the view that the contemporary diversity in family and household patterns is a threat to our way of life, argue that such a policy must promote equality and choice. It must develop public and community-based services which link public and private spheres. They argue that mothers should be able to make decisions about work, remarriage or cohabitation from a position of strength and self-reliance – not from emotional or economic dependency – and thus act in their child's best interests. Family policy should put children first, and work with the grain of social and familial change. Men's reponsibility should be emotional as well as financial and authoritarian. Successful family life is based on interdependence and social rights rather than isolated, private individualism.

This vision is one I shall return to in the later part of the book, when I consider how family centres and family policies could both support families and promote opportunities for their constituent members: children, women, men. But family centres need also to be understood as a response to the challenge from both the Left and the Right in the 1980s, in the UK and other western countries, to develop new forms of welfare which are less reliant on institutions, professional power, passive consumption. The challenge is not restricted to family and childcare services: Oliver (1990), writing of disability, argues that:

> The key issue for the future as far as the left is concerned is whether the 'crisis in' the welfare state can be resolved by offering users of services choice and control . . . It should be possible to allow for choice and control in service provision . . . if consumers have social rights to these services and if there are mechanisms whereby the needs of groups and communities . . . can be articulated by them . . . . (Oliver, 1990: 98–100)

'Choice', of course, is part of the Conservatives' rhetoric of the 1980s and 1990s: somehow greater consumer rights are presumed to lead to improved services if these are provided in a mixed economy of care. The Left and Centre ground (e.g. the Labour Party's Citizen's Charter [1991] or the Wagner Report [1988]) have also taken up the issue of consumers' rights, arguing for better choice and legal redress, and the key social policy initiatives of the 1980s – *Caring for People: Community care in the next decade and beyond* (DOH, 1989) (leading to the NHS and Community Care Act) and the 1989 Children Act – have both established complaints procedures for users and a greater sense of choice between a variety of services. Yet if the services are provided at only a minimal level in the first place, then a complaints procedure, or a right to choice or information, cannot increase their effectiveness or range. The new consumerist approach is one that limits citizenship to individual rights. Neither the Children Act nor the NHS and Community Care Act spells out exactly *how* services are to be delivered in the mixed economy, nor do they lay down a duty on government to provide resources to meet demand or need. Service provision and its quality, then, will depend on a complex interaction of civil service guidance notes and local authorities' attempts to prioritize and ration within groups of children 'in need' (Tunstill, 1991). Under these circumstances, will 'in need' become a status as stigmatizing as 'in Care', the status it was designed to replace? Will social workers' work focus – as it has done over the last century – around making such assessments? (Packman and Jordan, 1991).

Family centres are well placed to contribute to local resources, to provide some services and to help people create or argue for others – indeed, many are established to this end. However, the stress on *family* (why aren't they called *community* or *children's* centres?) contains an ideological message about the way in which caring in the community and social reproduction are to be carried out. For the present, minimalism in social provision underpins policy and practice: the challenge to family centres is whether they can be creative in that social context. Before we return to this challenge, we will look at how family centres work, and at their ideological roots.

CHAPTER 2

FAMILY CENTRES OBSERVED

Family centres provide services for families in need. Their common aims are to strengthen such families in the care of their children. Because poor families have been most vulnerable to having their children go into local authority Care and have been the main users of statutory and voluntary welfare services, family centres take their clientele from areas of social deprivation. Before the 1989 Children Act their aims were predominantly to prevent children going into 'voluntary' or court-ordered Care. Now the former category is obsolete, and family centres are enshrined in the Act as one of the means by which local authorities should carry out their duty to support families with community-based facilities, to provide daycare for children in need, and possibly to provide accommodation for children and young people. They could also be the setting in which access between children and their parents can be promoted where they have been separated, and they could provide the community facilities which must have been tried before a court can make an order.

Family centres are often managed by social workers and run by local authority social services departments or voluntary child welfare organizations which receive funding from their local authorities, central government and charitable donations. The activities and services of these centres include crèches, nursery groups, daycare, parent education (or parentcraft), adult education classes, keep fit, cookery, welfare rights, psychotherapy, counselling, group therapy, family therapy, self-help groups, health education, clinics and sessions for handicapped children. Many family centres have developed from day nurseries and children's homes which have begun to involve parents in the care of the children; others are like community centres with a focus on children. Family centres, then, are not all alike: the most obvious variations I observed were in the ways in which families participated in (and reached) the centre, whether social work or community work was the dominant approach, and the ways in which child abuse and family stress were conceptualized.

I shall describe some examples of family centres, before going on to make some comparisons between the centres in order to highlight similarities and differences. I shall draw both on the ten family centres which I observed and on those which have been well documented or discussed in others' research. Table 2.1 shows the centres I observed and the models they represented.

Table 2.1 Family centres in the research

		Type /model /focus			
Statutory/ local authority	Origins	Social work/ child protection/ client focused	Neighbourhood/ Community development	Service	Type of involvement and participation
Oaklands	Children's home/day nursery	√			Supervised
The Elm	Day nursery	√		√	Autonomous
The Ash	Day nursery	√		√	Autonomous
The Orchard	Children's home	√			Supervised
Grove Place	Children's home/day nursery	√			Supervised
Field Street	Day nursery	√			Supervised
Voluntary					
St John's	Day nursery		√	√	Autonomous
Meadow	Day nursery	√			Supervised
St Michael's	Children's home	√			Supervised
Market	Children's home	√			Supervised

Models which practitioners and professionals have delineated will be reviewed, and compared with the main factors which in my view produce differences between family centres: the relative autonomy of the professionals working in the centres, the policies of the local authority social services department, the enterprise of the voluntary childcare organizations, and low public commitment to daycare for young children. The social work of family centres will be further discussed in Chapter 5; here 'social work' is used in a loose sense: not all the family centre workers are qualified social workers – many are nursery nurses, some are community workers – but their methods and their 'parent' organizations are in a broad social work field, and families usually reach them via social workers' referrals.

The range of family centres

Oaklands Family Centre

Oaklands is a social services department family centre in a shire county in the south of England: situated on the outskirts of a large town with high unemployment it is far from the most needy areas it serves and its users are collected by bus. The reason for its location lies in the fact that it grew from a former children's home that developed into a day nursery and then a family centre in 1983. Its aims are not just to care for abused, neglected and impoverished children but to 'change parents' behaviour' and to prevent reception into Care and dependence on social workers. Daycare places were phased out and the numbers of children reduced in order to accommodate parents, with up to six families attending on any one day. All families (the majority being single mothers) are referred to the centre by social workers or health visitors: there is a commitment to honesty between staff and parents as to the reasons for referral and the purpose of attendance. Usually a contract or agreement is made to specify for how long, during what hours, and what activities the family will attend. Activities include counselling, discussion on child development and behaviour, and some social activities and outings.

The project organizer, trained in community work, is keen to demystify professional 'expertise'. His staff are not highly qualified (they are mainly nursery nurses) and they emphasize simple, practical help and advice with childcare. Nevertheless, the social services department organized training sessions on psychodynamic group-work and family therapy methods, and this ethos, together with an increasing focus and priority on working with children 'at risk' of abuse, now dominates the centre. The project organizer, while stressing the apparent effectiveness of these methods, nevertheless dislikes the high boundary which they impose on the centre by restricting the clientele to those who are referred with behavioural and psychological problems. These problems are not confined to child abuse, but include long-term difficulties in achieving 'normal' standards of family life and childcare and 'dependence' on social workers. The project organizer would prefer more general access to the centre by the existing clientele, and by others in their families and networks such as grandparents and teenagers, and he is developing an open crèche one morning a week. He would therefore like to reduce stigma, and to use the centre as far as possible as a resource for local people, but also to rehabilitate problem families to the 'natural' community of informal mutual aid.

Oaklands is a fairly representative example of a social-work/child protection family centre; although they vary considerably, the main areas of work – on children at risk of reception into Care, on child protection, and with families (often single mothers) in poverty – are core features. Before moving to a discussion of these features and attempting to draw up a typology or system of classication, I shall give two examples of centres in the voluntary sector, with the aim of demonstrating the diversity of family centres.

St John's Community and Daycare Centre

This project in south London is run by a major childcare voluntary organization which, like the other big voluntary organizations, began moving into new forms of childcare during the 1970s when their legacy of large institutions was outmoded. It runs a variety of centres in different cities – some focusing on social work and child protection, some, like St John's, more akin to community nurseries.

St John's was established in 1977. It is based in a very dilapidated church hall where daycare is provided for thirty-three local children. The play area is bright and lively, but poorly heated with battered furniture and equipment. Small staff rooms and a kitchen-dining room lead off the hall. The project leader considers the standard of accommodation to be unacceptably low and is pressing the voluntary organization for extensive refurbishment, or – preferably – a new building.

All the children come to St John's because their parents want them to come, and there is a long waiting list. Though many children are referred by social workers because they are in need, the centre workers take this to mean poor housing or poverty, or a parent's need to work: children are not taken on criteria of poor parenting or risk of abuse. Many of the children, who are mainly of Afro-Caribbean origin, come from extremely poor homes, and during the winter may arrive suffering from cold and hunger. Most of the parents work, or are students, and the nursery staff are sympathetic to the efforts they make to provide for their children: long hours of daycare are available if necessary. Thus, while the nursery staff would like to talk more to parents about their children, they consider it unrealistic to demand too much involvement. There are no time limits on attendance, and it is considered beneficial to the child to provide a stable and enriching environment until he or she reaches school age.

Non-working parents are welcome in the nursery, as helpers or just as people needing company; one father helps regularly in this way. The staff give practical help to parents – information on welfare rights and legal advice – and have an obvious sympathy for them. A community worker is based at the centre, encouraging a variety of local activities for families, youth and the elderly in the area. The centre and these projects reflect the Afro-Caribbean culture of the area in their staffing, diet and interests. The centre's staff and users share the same view of St John's as a service for local people, providing compensatory daycare for children and enabling parents to work in order to escape poverty. Parents participate in the centre as and how they wish, and are viewed by staff as equal, autonomous partners in the care of the children. Staff view family problems as resulting from poverty and racism, and see the centre as a resource to combat these.

The Walcot Centre

This was not a centre I observed, but I describe it as it is a well-documented example of a neighbourhood centre, with a strong emphasis on community development (Holman, 1988; Phelan, 1983). The Walcot Centre (its real name) was established in Swindon in 1979 as a joint initiative between the Children's Society, Wiltshire social services and education departments, and the Thamesdown Borough Council. It is neighbourhood-based due to the influence of the Thamesdown community development officer, who was also an Anglican clergyman with an interest in the Children's Society's plans for family centres. He brought together a headteacher with spare room at her infants' school and an interest in parental involvement, and a working party on the needs of the under-5s which had recommended support facilities for families on the lines of the Swindon Family Centre established by a group of mothers in 1974. Walcot was identified as an area of high social need – an estate developed in the 1950s, it had few facilities:

> The aim of the project is to identify and provide a flexible response to changing needs of the area. The overall aim is to improve the quality of life for residents on the estate by complementing the work of other agencies. (Thamesdown Voluntary Services Centre, n.d.: 32)

The ultimate aim was to enable more families to help themselves and others by providing additional support for existing networks of groups and thus, by maximizing resources in the area, preventing and alleviating stress in families. The work therefore focused on parent–child relationships *and* on community networks.

The centre is based in the school, comprising a nursery class run by the education department and a range of activities managed by the Children's Society and funded by Urban Aid grants. The centre is staffed by a project leader (a social worker), a community worker, a nursery teacher, a family project worker, and clerical and cleaning staff. Participation by local people is encouraged both in running activities and on the committee, and all the activities, with the exception of the welfare rights and coffee mornings, were set up at the request of local people. The activities range from problem-focused work (family counselling, family therapy, a Portage scheme for handicapped children, advice sessions) to preventive and supportive work (nursery classes, a crèche, playschemes, adult social activities and classes, outings, an unemployed group, keep fit, a tenants' association, a boys' club, and so on).

Common and different features of family centres

As we have already seen, family centres vary. How may we compare them? While stressing the two major variables – the means of public access, and professional ideologies and methods – family centres can be said to fall somewhere between the following poles:

Social-work/child protection centre	or	**Community development/ neighbourhood centre**
Families referred	or	Accessibility to the public
Strong boundary	or	Weak, permeable boundary
Deficit model – parental inadequacy requiring treatment	or	Opportunity model – parents need resources and services
Instrumental, goal-orientated activities	or	Expressive activities – broad range of activities
Activities determined by professionals	or	User determines choice of activities
Time limits on use of centre	or	Open-ended use of centre
Hierarchy and professional dominance strong	or	User participation in management of centre and activities
Social distance between staff and users	or	Informality, little social distance
Strong focus on parental role	or	Range of success roles (e.g. student, worker, activist)
Gender-blind	or	Focus on women's issues
Clientele drawn from similar social groups	or	Variety of social groups using the centre
Parental responsibility	or	Stress on support
Psychotherapeutic and behavioural methods such as	or	Community work and educational methods, client-

| family therapy; parentcraft | | centred counselling; advice-giving |
| Psychopathological and family dysfunction explanations | or | Ecological, personal *and* environmental reasons for stress |

The service model: The Elm Family Centre

Later in this chapter I shall consider professionals' models of family centres. Broadly, these consist of the client-centred (which I have called the social-work/child protection) centre, the neighbourhood centre, and community development centres. I concur with these models, but consider it important to add a fourth (adapted from Walker, 1991): the service centre. Only the service centre is based on the assumption that the centre provides a service which directly benefits the users, that the service is one which they freely choose and in which they participate as much or as little as they wish. It presupposes that the staff see their task as providing a professional service, including daycare, counselling and health education, and that the centre is more than a space to facilitate activities or to work on referred families. It is closest to the neighbourhood model and to community nurseries, but it emphasizes a professional (rather than, for instance, self-help groups) service. It includes a commitment to daycare services, to the sharing of caring tasks between state and family, and at present it is rarely to be found. Some London social services department family centres in Labour-controlled boroughs – with, in the mid-1980s, a relatively good range of social and health services in their areas (for instance specialist clinics at teaching hospitals, extensive nursery education, more established self-help projects) – were able to adopt this approach. St John's, described above, and the Elm Centre were able to stress daycare for children combined with the provision of opportunities to women for education or employment. The daycare they provided was child-centred and available for as long as was wanted by parent(s) and child(ren), usually until school entry, but parents could join activities at the centre if they wished, and were encouraged to do so.

The Elm Family Centre is in purpose-built accommodation, part of a modern estate in inner London. It is a large centre, with sixty daycare places for children, though staff shortages mean that these are not all taken. Physically it is well integrated with the flats which surround it and has a pleasant atmosphere, with good play equipment and furnishings. It was originally designed as a conventional day nursery, but in the early 1970s the matron retired, the building was renovated, and a new organizer with both social-work and nursery nursing qualifications was appointed.

The centre is open from 8 a.m. to 5.30 p.m. to suit working parents, although during my observation only one parent was working full-time. Most parents are single or unsupported, and some are very young; several work 'on the side'. The organizer aimed to make the centre a 'therapeutic environment', not a treatment centre, so that usually parents can choose how to use the time available to them while their child is there. Some enjoy the company; others want time for themselves. However, since most children are referred to the centre by social workers and health visitors because they have severe problems – whether of emotional or material kinds – plans are made with parents clarifying its purpose and nature. Contracts are rarely used, as compulsory attendance is considered incompatible with the philosophy that the parents should be attracted to the centre and want to come – for instance, by offering practical resources such as sewing machines or health or welfare rights advice. Grandparents or other significant relatives and siblings can drop in. The centre staff make a point of tolerating 'just sitting and gossiping', as they accept that the parents – predominantly mothers – have stressful lives, and that mutual support and acceptance by staff is helpful. However, they encourage parents to involve themselves in social events, fund-raising, and outings through the parents' association. The staff also hold group discussions on aspects of caring for and managing children, and the topics tend to be suggested by parents. The staff use their group-work skills to involve the shyer mothers, and to prevent a vocal group from dominating activities.

In this centre the staff felt that they were taking 'heavier' cases than they had been taking a few years previously. They felt that families' problems were worsening because of poor housing, poor recreation and play facilities, and the racism and marginalization experienced by the local Asian community. While these difficulties appeared to be producing more children who were abused or at risk of abuse, the staff felt that the environmental problems were the real issue, and that the parents could manage their difficult lives better with some undemanding support and with compensatory care for their children. The centre tries to avoid stigmatizing the families by being as open as possible to the community, with youth clubs and the local tenants' association allowed to use its rooms in the evenings, and a crèche with play sessions alongside the full-time daycare.

All the centres I observed were working with broadly similar parents: lone motherhood, unemployment, benefit claims, and poor housing dogged their lives. Staff and institutional perception of 'family stress' varied with the openness of the centres. The social-work/child protection centres viewed child abuse as an individual product of disturbed family relationships, whereas the community development/neighbourhood/service centres viewed it as a product of lack of opportunities and of social isolation. The service model offers daycare or health education or social space as social rights to users rather than as treatment for pathologized individuals. The danger of the social work model is that it (often unintentionally) reinforces the notion of the self-reliant and responsible family which does not resort to state services except in extreme situations.

Research on family centres: professionals' assessments and models

I shall use the term 'professionals' to refer to social workers and managers of family centres and to those whose work is connected with family centres, either in research and development terms or managerially – that is to say, people who are of the family centre world. Professionals' classifications of centres have centred around the following factors: the relationship between users and centre; the range of social groups using the centre: views of family deviance; professional orientation of staff; and the roots or origin of the centre.

The relationship with the clientele reflects the function of the centre: neighbourhood and community development *or* child protection (Adamson and Warren, 1983). Phelan (1983) distinguishes the community-work from the social-work orientation, identifying the community-work model with the absence of contractual obligations. By this she means that the contract with social services departments to provide a daycare or child protection service militates against the greater informality and lesser social distance between staff and users that is found in the community-work model. Similarly, Birchall (1982) contrasts two 'extremes of a continuum of practice': first, the 'drop-in' centre, open for mothers and children to use as often as they like, when they like, and how they like; second, the centre for high-risk families, used by families referred by social workers and attending at specified times for specified purposes. In the drop-in community centre model the clientele have made their own judgement about using the centre; in the social-work–child protection centre the judgement has been made on their behalf (but usually with the user's 'agreement') by social workers. The clientele therefore has more autonomy in its relationship with the community-work model than with the social-work–child protection model, which has restrictions on use and a narrow range of clients.

Warren's (1990) national survey of family centres (with responses from 75 per cent of the total of 495) revealed the degree to which child protection work has come to dominate family centres: 'The study concludes that most family centres serve as a function of the local authorities' apparatus for child protection, where investigation and assessment are main objectives' (abstract). Child protection was a major function in at least 70 per cent of centres, and their daycare, though provided in 49 per cent, appeared to fulfil parentcraft or assessment goals (i.e. child protection goals) rather than the traditional child-centred format. These findings were as true of voluntary- as of statutory-sector family centres. Adamson and Warren, Birchall, and Phelan argue that it is child protection responsibilities which propel family centres from the open, neighbourhood type to a social-work type, with less general participation, a narrower range of activities, and more restricted user groups. However, while all the ten centres observed in the present research had some responsibility for child protection, some allowed parents to come and go as they wished; some gave primary care and attention to the children; some insisted on parental attendance on specific behavioural programmes, or family therapy or counselling.

Sociological research on institutions has shown that it is not so much severity of residents' impairment or difficulty that determines the boundaries between the institution and outside world, the degree of social distance between staff and residents, or the flexibility of routines and timetables, as staff training, attitudes, beliefs and culture, and the traditions of the organization (King *et al.*, 1975; Milham *et al.*, 1975; Tizard *et al.*, 1975). Professionals' perceptions of the causes of family deviance therefore affect the work of family centres. Luckock (1986) contrasts the deficit with the opportunity model, echoing Bernstein's (1971) distinction between regulative and constitutive schooling. In the deficit model, family failure at the psychological level is the focus of family work. By contrast, parenting problems can be viewed as normal but exacerbated by lack of resources – friends, relatives, good housing – so that in the opportunity model 'the response is to tap wider resources'. Increasing resources to the family may include psychotherapeutic work, daycare, health and other education, and social and political pressure to improve the environment while emphasizing parents' responsibility for effecting change with these new resources. Professionals' perceptions will depend on their orientation – within social work, community work, family therapy and childcare are all segments which to some extent have competed with each other in the family centre field (see Chapter 5).

Birchall draws this diversity of approaches together by noting that raising mothers' self-esteem, considered the best way of improving children's lives, was the common aim, but different methods were used in attempting to achieve this:

> although traditional pre-school activities were provided for the children, specific support to mothers assumed an important part of the work. This was mainly based on the belief that if the mother could raise her feelings of self-esteem, then the relationship with her child would improve. (There appeared to be little involvement of fathers, although some centres provided activities in which they could take part.) (Birchall, 1982: 19)

The relative power of professionals and clientele are of major concern in understanding the observed variations between the centres. It is characteristic of the neighbourhood centres and of some social-work centres that the staff sought to disperse power to the users – either through therapies designed to give individuals greater control over and awareness of their own lives, or through the unconditional offering of services such as daycare. The centres had different ideas of what participation meant, and it was noticeable that the local authority family centres – which have broadly similar aims and conditions, including a child protection mandate – nevertheless had different attitudes to parental involvement: some stressed the social benefit of daycare as a service and sought to involve a range of community groups.

Centres can also be classified by their development. Phelan points to the origins of centres in day nurseries, residential children's homes, community centres, or self-help organizations. These origins affect and colour the subsequent form of the centre. Staff background, training and ideology cut through this, as do the principles and objectives of the broader funding and managing organizations, so that moral reform, psychotherapy, and practical services may more or less easily coexist – a point noted by Archard (1979) in his study of agencies in the vagrancy and alcoholism field. Voluntary organizations, which have been extremely active in the family centre sphere, have their own traditions, and have responded to the changing social policy climate in different ways (see below). Centres, then, are not only different from each other, but they can be *internally* diverse, perhaps even contradictory. Perhaps it is most useful to consider the tensions between types as characteristic of social welfare in the UK. Walker (1991) stresses this in her distinction between *direct service provision* and the *treatment-orientated approach*:

> Tensions can exist within family centres between direct service provision and a treatment or therapeutic orientation. Service provision recognising that parenting is a demanding, isolating and stressful experience, encompasses activities intended to provide support. These might include advice, day care, toy libraries, discussion groups, creches – any service parents choose to use. In contrast a treatment-oriented approach targets particular parents or families identified as requiring surveillance, monitoring and some change. Attendance may be compulsory (or veiled compulsion); parents may therefore be ambivalent towards the opportunities presented by the centre and anxious about the stigma of attending. (Walker, 1991: 60)

Holman (1988), having surveyed Children's Society and some other voluntary-sector family centres, arrived at three models, all of which he places in the frame of preventive work:

The client-focused model

This has specialized activities; most resources are devoted to one service and one client category – usually care, therapy and training for the under-5s and their parents. Clients are referred, usually from social workers in the statutory social services department, on grounds of neglectful or abusive care or the risk of these. The centre admits only certain clients, and local residents are not expected to walk in. The running of the centre is in the hands of qualified staff rather than local residents or their committees; it combines highly skilled family support with the danger of stigma – 'it's where the battered children go'.

The neighbourhood model

This has a broad range of activities: a variety of activities used by different age groups, and people with different interests from the entire neighbourhood. It has an open door, and encourages people to drop in. The centre is for the neighbourhood, not for the statutory services. There is an emphasis on local participation, with a high level of involvement by residents in the running of the centre. There are flexible staff roles: project staff could act as service providers, running clubs, or as counsellors, or as stimulators supporting self-run groups, and it may be hard to distinguish between staff and volunteers.

The community development model

Some project staff commented that the emphasis within the neighbourhood approach on staff directly providing services lessened the reponsibilities given to residents. The alternative was what they called the community development model. The project leader at the Millmead Neighbourhood Centre explained it thus:

> We have a community development philosophy. We are trying to enable people to exercise more power over their lives and to enable them to develop facilities and activities which benefit them and their families . . . . (Holman, 1988: 165)

This model shares the broad range of activities – the open door, neighbourhood identification and local participation – with the neighbourhood model. It also includes a commitment to collective action and a hope that residents might act collectively to improve the quality of their lives.

As Holman noted, 'In reality the three types of project overlapped, and, indeed, one project might contain elements of all three models' (1988: 166). Given the continual process of negotiation which takes place between professions (and different segments of each profession), between professionals and their wider organization, its management and wider leadership, as well as the *local* politics of negotiations between agencies, segments of professions, user groups, and so forth, one could not expect centres to settle into fixed types, or that certain types of organization (social services departments, community groups, church voluntary organizations) would run centres of a certain type.

I suggested some dimensions of family centres above, and while ideal-type centres would fall into one side of the dimensions or the other, in fact most have features from each side or operate in a tension between each side. In many centres the social workers wanted more of a service model – ideally to have a centre with several different types of services available to a range of groups, such services being based on professional skills as well as a commitment to user empowerment and participation, but restrictions in local authority budgets meant that this was a pipe dream. They had to turn from the service/social benefit approach to something more targeted or concentrated on referred families, or more based on self-help. In reality, then, there is considerable blurring between models, often because of lack of resources and the way that lack has shaped options in this marketplace of ideas. To explore this further, I shall now turn to two church voluntary organizations and look at the kinds of centres they have developed and their part in the debates on social welfare, children and the family.

Voluntary organizations and family centres

The voluntary organizations began establishing family projects in the community in the mid 1970s, and Warren's (1990) national survey found that they were running 42.5 per cent of family centres. This has been predominantly a response to the decline in the use of their children's homes after the large social services departments were created in 1971. Moreover the birth rate declined, and the numbers of young children fell from a peak in 1972 (Parker, 1980). 'Rescue' was no longer fashionable, and the voluntary organizations needed a new role (see Chapter 1). Sir Keith Joseph's invitation to find ways of 'breaking the cycle of deprivation', the New Right's concern with the 'crisis' in the family (see Chapter 4), and the left-wing Community Development Projects and Urban Programme all offered new scope for participative, family-centred, self-help community work (Holman, 1988). How did the National Children's Home and the Church of England Children's Society respond to these challenges? What kind of family centres did they develop?

The National Children's Home

The National Children's Home (NCH) is based on Christian values and linked to the Methodist Church. Founded in 1869, as its name implies, it was conceived as an alternative to large institutions, aiming to provide residential *homes* for destitute and 'orphaned' children. Like the other voluntary children's organizations, it was forced to reconsider its role in the 1960s and 1970s, and NCH now sees itself as recapturing the reforming role of the original organization, a role which was muted in the middle years of this century. Now it runs projects which strive to prevent family breakdown and are targeted on children at risk in deprived areas. These projects promote family life, often through parent education, parentcraft, and family life education. Like the other big voluntary organizations it appointed a social policy adviser in the 1970s in order to take advantage of changing government thinking on the state–voluntary relationship and to promote projects in line with new initiatives on opportunities for volunteering and preventive childcare services. The NCH is explicit on its Christian values; a 1983 social-work policy paper stated commitment to the United Nations Declaration on the Rights of the Child, and to Christian principles of forgiveness, love and shared accountability.

The NCH might offer opportunities for participation and volunteering by local people, but its projects are staffed by professionals, and there is a commitment to training and further professionalization: the projects themselves – especially those which work with 'at risk' children – are controlled by professional social workers. At the NCH conference on family centres in 1981, its Discussion Document emphasized poor parenting as the main reason for children needing social services and family centres:

> It follows then that unless the home situation and quality of care can be improved the effects of any centre-based help given to children are going to be limited. If the home situation and patterns of parental care are going to be influenced to the benefit of the child it equally follows that direct on-going involvement with the parents is essential to the work of the centre . . . .

The document stressed social work as appropriate for damaged mothers and as the best way of helping children, and viewed such intervention as necessary to break cycles and patterns of poor parenting. Tom White, a former director of a social services department, was NCH social work director at the time of the research. In an interview (*Community Care*, 23 May 1985) he underlined his working-class origins, his Labour Party and Low Church background, and also his commitment to social-work professionalism. He displays, then, a concern for traditional family life, combined with a commitment to social reform and a Fabian respect for the professions.

The four London NCH family centres are part-funded by their local authorities to provide daycare and services for children. The centres vary; one provides family places alongside its day nursery, offering a 'therapeutic environment to families in chaos', as well as facilities to community groups and families who want to use them, a women's group, and a Portage scheme for handicapped children. The feminist ethos of that centre is in stark contrast to that of the Meadow Family Centre (not its real name).

The Meadow Family Centre opened in 1975, when it provided daycare for six children of working parents. In 1982 a social worker was attached to the staff, and she changed the emphasis to working with parents. At the same time the centre expanded to take sixteen children; while it continues to be a registered nursery, it now takes families referred as in need or 'at risk' by the local authority social workers and health visitors. The centre is behind a very large Victorian redbrick Methodist church; its small doorway is hard to detect beneath the enveloping church. The accommodation is extremely cramped and dilapidated: although efforts have been made to brighten the walls, it clearly needs major renovation, and many would not consider it suitable for a nursery. The children squeeze round tables in the kitchen at mealtimes. They have one large playroom with plenty of playthings. The children are all black or of mixed race. A new social worker on the staff has developed group-work amongst the parents, and a speech therapist, physiotherapist, GP, child psychiatrist and psychiatric social worker visit weekly or fort- nightly, the latter two acting as consultants to the staff.

The centre is open for children from 10 a.m. to 4 p.m. Older children who were previously at the nursery can come after school. There is also a crèche and a childminders' group. Parents and their children attend on 'contract' and are expected to follow a range of activities designed and monitored by their keyworker to 'meet their needs'. They may have play sessions with their child, individual counselling, welfare rights advice, and group discussions. The play sessions may be held in the families' own houses. The plan for the future is that a place with a childminder will follow the centre's programme, and that the staff will do more outreach work – for instance in clinics and playgroups, and by developing their childminders' group. 'Parents', then, means mothers at this centre, but there is little sympathy for the working mother or for a woman-centred approach: the project organizer said that the centre should not be part of 'a separation that may lead to problems in the child relating to its parent later on'. Roughly 80 per cent of the mothers are single or unsup- ported, and are considered to be problem families rather than simply unemployed. For the mothers in the area there is no nursery that would take children full-time if they did want to work, and despite a possible stigma hanging over the centre, mothers knock on the door asking for daycare places, hoping to be able to work.

Because the centre was started as a day nursery, and because each family now has its own pattern of attendance, confusion can arise amongst users about its function. This is to some extent perpetuated at official level, for while the annual report on the centre (which goes to the local authority and the NCH head- quarters) stresses child protection as a major aspect of its work, we find something different being said to parents in publicity leaflets:

> The families presently attending the family centre do so for a variety of reasons which include language and developmental delay, behaviour difficulties, stress in the family, etc. We also have a very limited number of places for children whose parents are engaged in work or study.

The vaguely defined aims of such projects can be seen to lie in the dilemma in which the voluntary organizations find themselves – wanting the prestige and role the Conservatives would give them, yet continuing to argue for social justice and for meeting social need. Yet within the NCH's own ideology there is a contradictory blend of social reformism and individualistic moral conservatism. In its projects this is revealed in the focus on the individual family, its pathology, its ungendered use of the term 'parent' when women's lives are the issue. Yet the workers in some centres have challenged this, showing that organizations do not dictate practice: the front-line workers negotiate the way in which their role and tasks may be interpreted and carried out. However, the organization's focus on the traditional home and family is unequivocal (e.g. Barritt, 1979). The family-in-crisis is a theme it has eagerly developed (we shall develop this theme further in Chapter 4).

In its recent thinking on the kinds of family centres it should promote, the NCH has stressed the open integrated model, and a move away from the closed, therapeutic kind. It sees this as a model which combines elements of the client-focused (social work/child protection) and neighbourhood models:

> The advantages of this model are that open services are less likely to stigmatize those who use them. There is also a strong likelihood that stress factors and actual or potential abuse are identified at an early stage. Research has demonstrated that these open centres do reach a higher proportion of vulnerable families . . . nevertheless client focused work should take place in all of them [the centres]. Similarly whilst not necessarily being defined as an integrated model all centres are involved in the complex task of integrating structured development work with children, educational partnership work with parents and collaborative

relationships with other agencies. (NCH document on Family Centre policy, 1991: 4)

The NCH now takes as key principles paramountcy of the child's welfare (cf. the Children Act 1989), parental responsibility, anti-discrimination, reciprocity, and empowerment (as opposed to marginalization and stigmatization). The problems with this approach lie in the poor general level of services against which it is set: can poor families be responsible for the same levels of childcare without the resources or services available to middle class families?

The Church of England Children's Society

The Children's Society was founded in 1881 by Edward Rudolph, an Anglican who was later ordained. He originally established homes for 'waifs and strays', gaining the support of the highest officials of the Church. He pioneered the small 'family' group home, fostering and boarding out, and, like Barnardo, the emigration of children to the colonies (principally Canada and Australia – Wagner, 1982). The post-war welfare state reduced demand for the organization's services, as did later changes in attitude to abortion and illegitimacy, which reduced the numbers of children for adoption or permanent care. By the 1970s it had to rethink its role or risk disappearance, so it turned to preventive work with children and families, to community work and specialist childcare work (Holman, 1988; Phelan, 1983).

Holman has done much to promote the community work of the Children's Society. He has argued that in their projects the workers should try to break the client–worker relationship of traditional social work, which in his view results in people becoming unable to do things for themselves. The Children's Society workers he describes as 'resourceful friends' tied to local people by 'bonds of emotion' (Holman, 1983: 70). Christian community workers emphasize participation to avoid passivity and stigma, and the promotion of solidarity through the 'gifts of self'. This is a different kind of altruism from that analysed by Titmuss (1970) in his study of blood donation which, in the UK, is characterized by voluntary *anonymous* giving. Titmuss argued that voluntary donation fostered social integration and participation in social welfare as well as the dissemination of superior ethical values based on altruism. What is at the heart of this altruism, however, is a self*less* giving, the relationship between strangers – or, more precisely, no relationship at all.

Voluntary welfare organizations, by contrast, stress the personal bonds between giver and receiver, or organizer and participant. This personal relationship is at the heart of welfare schemes such as Home-Start, which will be discussed in Chapter 4, as well as statutory social work, and it marks their difference from the more bureaucratic and impersonal format of medical or business encounters. The Children's Society has been particularly assertive in stressing the right of all to give – in order to redress the power implicit or explicit in most social-work relationships – and it emphasizes participation as a means of making this possible by preventing the marginalization of welfare recipients. Holman and Halser, who have dominated much of the thinking behind Children's Society projects, have insisted that 'The issue for staff in Family Centres is not just what to do, but how to enable people "to do" for themselves'(Hasler, 1984: 3). This approach was central to the Family Centre Project in Melbourne, a project which strongly influenced Children's Society policies in the UK in the late 1970s. The Melbourne project aimed to combat the entrenched poverty of families by maximizing their power over resources, decision-making, relationships and information in the centre. The general principle was deprofessionalization, so that the staff gradually handed over responsibility for the project to the families. Participation was the method by which families learnt organizing skills and overcame their years of passivity (Liffman, 1978).

Holman's account of the Children's Society family centres says:

> Whatever the differences, they were outweighed by the similarities. All the centres were accessible to their communities. The buildings were located in the midst of the neighbourhoods they wished to serve. Moreover, they were accessible in the sense that people would walk in without negotiating receptionists and with no need to make appointments. Further, although the projects did have differences of emphasis in their activities, certain services were common to all. All ran groups for mothers and toddlers, offered welfare rights advice and were prepared to give time to

individuals. Again, each project had an underlying belief in local involvement, in encouraging residents to identify with the project and to take a part in running it. Above all, there was a unity of purpose in that all the centres gave priority to strengthening families, to improving the quality of parenting and to enabling children to stay within their own families and neighbourhoods. (Holman, 1983: 9)

Family centres and participation

Family centres generally make a link between the quality of individual families' lives and the community and networks those families live in. Because of this link, preventive work is equated with community development work, the encouragement of participatory activities and the support and development of informal networks to increase individuals' resources and self-esteem and to reduce isolation and alienation.

Participation is not only an aim, then, but a method: it is assumed that if parents are provided with opportunities to be members of groups, they will gain in self-esteem, will realize that they have something to give in helping others, become more socially skilled, and form friendships and other sustaining relationships. Yet we have seen that in different family centres parents participate in different ways, and that in the same centre, people may participate on different conditions. This latter point can cause tensions: as Stones says of her centre (run by Barnardo's in Bristol), there can be stigmatization of one group by another, and:

> publicity has sometimes caused concern for users; for example, a local newspaper, when reporting on a visit of the President of Barnardo's, the Princess of Wales, to the centre, described it as helping people with social and emotional problems. A number of users were understandably angered by this limited account and there was a tendency for *drop-in* users to see such stigmatisation as caused by other groups such as *family group day* (i.e. the group with defined parenting difficulties) or the *prisoners' wives group*. Thus some groups may wish to emphasize their distinction from other groups at the centre. (Stones, 1989: 98, original emphasis.)

At nine out of the ten centres observed, families' access was mediated and determined by social workers' or health visitors' negotiations with the staff. Only St John's negotiated directly with parents wanting services. I therefore included details of the Walcot Centre because although it was not a centre that I observed, it is a good example of a centre which stresses openness to the public and (consequently) has a wide range of activities, users and groups, and participative management. The 'closed' centres have developed as they have partly from the scarcity of pre-school daycare (so that places become heavily rationed) but also because of rising anxiety in social services departments on the issue of effective child protection. All the family centres in the research were under pressure from social workers and health visitors to provide a treatment and monitoring service for families who had histories of child abuse or were perceived as 'at risk', and the strategy documents of local authorities described family centres as places for the monitoring, assessment, treatment and prevention of child abuse.

Heiser and Godfrey's (1984) research for the London Borough of Camden found that Council allocation and priority policies (whereby only the most stressed, depressed parents, possibly with children defined as 'at risk', gained Young Family Care Centre or day nursery places) confirmed stereotypes in the public mind that only families who are deviant or not coping attend centres and nurseries. There are parallels with the Downtown family centre in Rotherhithe in London which was established with an aim of maximizing local participation, but local residents resisted the project at first:

> out of a fear that the centre was to be for 'problem families' and that its existence would lead to the local authority concentrating such families in the area (Willmott and Mayne, 1983: 39)

The voluntary organizations' centres were under pressure because although they are formally independent, they receive a proportion of their funding from their local authorities' social services departments. They are included in these departments' strategy documents as part of the range of local child protection and preventive family services, so that social workers refer families in the same way as they would to social services department centres. This causes resentment, for the voluntary family centres feel that they may lose their autonomy in their field of work, and that the more community-orientated centres are being asked to work with dangerous and difficult people. Linthwaite (1982), for example, has described a Save the Children Fund family centre where disruptive families were referred by social workers from outside the area and were resented by local users. The project organizer at St Michael's, a Children's Society centre which concentrates on treatment of difficult families, was concerned about client dumping, estimating that 80–90 per cent of the users had been in prison, psychiatric hospital or other institutions, and that their work was becoming considerably heavier due to the lack of community care provision. A voluntary family centre in Swindon found that the local authority attempted to substitute the (cheaper) family centre for its own declining children's provision:

> the inadequate funding of the day nursery at the Swindon family centre, when many referrals have been received from social workers for children 'at risk', is at least a serious misuse of the project, given that any direct provision would have been much more expensive. (Thamesdown Voluntary Services Centre, n.d.: 4)

This situation of scarce daycare and community care services, rationing, and the more demanding work facing social workers, can produce a clash between social work and users' needs and values. When a centre has succeeded in drawing in local individuals and groups on the community development or neighbourhood model, the organizers may find that the users' participation becomes problematic: some users may wish to avoid 'contamination' by problem families, to discourage men from using the centre, or to resist anti-racist policies (Stones, 1989). There must be clear guidelines on the limits of parental involvement and the overall principles of the centre if this conflict is to be negotiated successfully and not to cause confusion and resentment amongst users who may be attending the centre on different conditions and bases.

I shall return to these in Chapter 6. Here I shall conclude by delineating two poles of participation which we find in family centres – though as we have seen, in reality there is a blurring:

individuals may move between these poles, centres may involve users on different bases, and so forth.

First, we may speak of involvement which stems from the professionals' desire to extend their effectiveness and influence beyond their usual 'target': for instance, the participation of parents in the care and treatment of handicapped children: the parent is a trusted auxiliary and an acknowledged and competent expert on the child. The involvement of parents in primary schools, especially in reading schemes, is another example. In terms of family centres, this type of involvement goes best with the service model: users might or might not be referred with a specific problem, but they consume, as citizens, a service they have chosen how to use. I call this pole *autonomous participation*.

Second, within the self-help model of service, such as play groups, parents cooperate to create mutually agreed services. The parents have equal social status to professionals in the childcare field and are articulate and well organized, to the extent that they may become semi-professionalized and contract services to or from the local state. Again we see autonomous participation, but where this model is put into practice in areas of deprivation it is under severe strain: residents may not have the personal, material or environmental resources to achieve the degree of self-help aimed for (Finch, 1984; Holman, 1985), and may prefer a professional service for their children to compensate for the deprivations of their lives. If such people are expected to provide childcare services out of their own resources, it seems to me that this should be characterized as *exploitative participation*. It is akin to neglect in the community, to mutual aid enforced by lack of services (Abrams, 1980), and as such is part of the process of the limitation of state commitment to social services. Family centres represent a decline in public care services and an attempt to make welfare-dependent families find alternatives. The lack of adequate community care services for elderly, disabled and mentally ill people has exacerbated the crisis for families and carers. So the work of family centres reflects the greater demands being made on 'responsible' families in the 1990s in Britain, and demands on social workers to make such policies work, or to step in when they do not.

The other pole is to be found where access is through social-work referrals, and the purpose of the referral is to address some sort of individual or family problem. Surveillance of the users becomes a condition of their receiving services, and it is the professional, not the client, who determines what those services shall be. Families are seen in terms of their defects or deprivation rather than their strengths. I call this pole *supervised involvement*. We should note that social workers in family centres often say they would prefer more autonomous participation, but shortage of resources of a general and universal nature, for families and children, pulls families into a narrow and targeted service. At the same time this pole reflects the more controlling style which came into social services departments in the 1980s, and the tendency to deter most calls on social services by concentrating only on the 'heavy end' of child protection work. It represents a withdrawal of social work from a wider brief of primary support services into targeted work with those 'at risk' or 'in need' (under the Children Act).

In later chapters I shall stress the service model and how it would look in family centres. In my view its marginalization reflects a general lack of commitment to good daycare policies for children and equal opportunities for women. While the Labour-controlled boroughs and some voluntary projects did try to promote this model during the 1980s, it is under threat in the UK, though common in other European countries. The reasons for this marginalization will be uncovered in the next three chapters, in which I shall excavate the origins of family centres. In the next two chapters we turn to the political roots of family centres, looking at the politics of childhood and the debates on family life.

CHAPTER 3

ROOTS OF FAMILY CENTRES
The politics of childhood

This chapter will review some of the debates and look at key actors in the field of childhood need. I shall argue that we must understand policy as an outcome of political pressure and manoeuvring by interested groups (philanthropic organizations, professions, and pressure groups) rather than as the expression of humanity, and that the real agenda of campaigns for children is not so much children's own needs as the continuous process of shaping and reforming the family, the supposedly pivotal institution in social reproduction and social order. I shall look at the campaigns of organizations such as the NSPCC, and thus the politics of child abuse and childcare, culminating in the implementation of the 1989 Children Act in 1991. This Act enshrines much of the thinking behind family centres and, like them, blends a certain traditionalism as to family responsibilities and privacy with a commitment to child protection. Chapter 4 also looks at children's policies and services but focuses on those that stress parental and maternal involvement, such as playgroups. In Chapters 5 and 6 I shall look at the practice implications of this contemporary policy: here we are concerned with politics and history.

Child saving and child protection

A political approach to policy analysis does not imply that organizations campaigning for the child lack integrity in their claims to represent humanitarian values. Rather, I shall argue that campaigns are selectively heard, that some reformers are ignored, and that therefore much abuse and need remains ignored (such as that of children in institutions in the last century [and this?], of children in poverty, or of children who suffer persecution and discrimination). Further, it must be noted that reform movements working to rescue or reform children have meant that often 'children, not their abusive guardians, felt the weight of the moral crusade. They, not their parents, were institutionalised' (Pfohl, 1977: 311). The contemporary 'crusade' may also not benefit children: no longer institutionalized, they may instead be repressively neglected in the community.

Child protectionist policies such as the United Nations Declaration on the Rights of the Child (1959) and the Convention on the Rights of the Child (1990) do not expand the child's world but protectively restrict him or her to the family, supposedly the 'natural' milieu of the developing child. This restriction of the child's world and the replacement of opportunities to work by the obligation to attend school remove independence and the chances of survival from many of the world's children (Ennew, 1986). Freeman (1983) has contrasted the liberationist impulse in the children's rights movement with the protectionist one of the child savers who would remove the child from the sphere of adult life. Hegar (1989) has delineated four approaches to childhood in Western society over the last century:

> Each approach has had periods of predominance in various countries, but all continue to influence thinking about the rights of juveniles, leading at times to confusion and to contradiction in policy. The three, in order of emergence, are: (1) the traditional approach, which holds that parents are the natural protectors of children and that independent rights for children are unnecessary; (2) the protective approach, which defines a regulatory and interventive role for society, particularly when parental protection is unfeasible or inadequate; and (3) the liberationist approach, which favours expanded rights for children to make inde-

pendent choices. In some countries, movements have begun in the past ten years to return to a stronger role for parents, a position that is best characterized as [4] neo-traditionalism. (Hegar, 1989: 108; (4)added to original)

The important fact is not the chronological sequence of these approaches, but the implications of the fact that contemporary society reflects the influence of all of them, and especially the emerging fourth, neo-traditionalism.

Child saving in the nineteenth century and early twentieth century

Child welfare organizations and legislation, and the profession of social work – in Europe and in the United States – have their roots in the late nineteenth century, although there is a longer history of provision for and control of children, dating from Tudor times. The campaigns on behalf of the factory and mining child in the first four decades of the nineteenth century drew attention to the appalling exploitation of children and began the process of removing them from the labour market, a process that was not completed until the introduction of compulsory schooling in 1880. While undoubtedly there was humanitarian concern with children's welfare in industry, historians have shown that much of the concern of reformers like Shaftesbury (or Oastler, Sadler, Kingsley or Disraeli) was with sexual morality and traditional family relationships.

> The employment of female children . . . has the effect of preventing them from acquiring the most ordinary and necessary knowledge of domestic management and family economy, that the young females in general . . . are nearly ignorant of the arts of baking and cooking, and, generally speaking entirely so of the use of the needle, that when they come to marry, the wife possesses not the knowledge to enable her to give to her husband the common comforts of a home . . . .

Thus was the conclusion of a subcommissioner of the 1842 Children's Employment Commission (quoted in Humphries,

1981: 17). The Tory radicals formed an 'alliance' with male trade unionists who also wanted an end to child labour – not just for humanitarian reasons, but to avoid being undercut by cheaper child and female labour. They pushed for a family wage, now conceived of not as the joint earnings of the family working as a team in industry but as those of the man alone, who would now be able to support his wife and children. But the issue was not just about this 'soft' side of the Victorian family ideal: there was a concern that if women and children earned their own living, they could exist quite independently of the man in their family and would have no grounds for accepting his authority.

The saving of the industrial child reflects a moral concern: the presence of women and children in industry was repeatedly linked to *their* depravity. The picture of vice and indecency in factories and mines was drawn as much to point to the dangers of a de-moralized working class (and thus the danger to the middle and upper classes) as to protest on behalf of child victims. Thus it was that the reforms which promoted education within the factory day boiled down to religious instruction (Henriques, 1979; Humphries, 1981; Pinchbeck and Hewitt, 1973). So while the campaigns to protect the industrial child were in many ways ahead of their time in their humanity and their rejection of unlimited exploitation (and were connected with the anti-slavery movement), they were also able to achieve some of their objectives because of an underlying conservatism and anxiety, shared with the dominant class, about the working-class family. Saving the child cannot be separated from saving the family: child welfare is interwoven with moral reform of the family (Behlmer, 1982).

The social purity campaigns of the late nineteenth century on prostitution, incest, and the age of consent were also 'successful' in so far as they too shared in the discourse and anxiety about the fragility of the working-class family, and the need to set clear norms of sexual and gender-role conduct in families of *all* classes. For it was not just the working class family that had been damaged by the forces of change, rapid industrialization and urban growth (Anderson, 1971): the upper classes came under strain from new rights for women in suffrage, education, divorce and property. A new companionate model of the conjugal relationship was constructed to replace what had been predominantly an economic partnership. Men's sexuality now had to be contained in the marriage relationship, and middle-class wives had to become responsive and sexualized (Jeffreys, 1985; Weeks, 1981). The social purity groups, while checking on 'vice', also raised uncomfortable issues of the 'rights' of men to exploit sexually their servants, children, girl prostitutes, unwilling wives: in raising norms of sexual conduct they participated in redrawing them in ways which were once again contained within the family and under male dominance. Out of this grew the new 'experts' in babycare and sex and marriage – experts like Truby King and Marie Stopes, with huge popular audiences from the 1920s onwards (Hardyment, 1983), and the infant welfare movement at the beginning of the twentieth century (Lewis, 1980) – and then in child guidance and marriage guidance, through to their equivalents today, of which family centres are an example.

I want briefly to mention nineteenth-century organizations whose primary concern was child rescue, for the practices and traditions of Barnardo's and the NSPCC have had a lasting impact on policy. The 1870s and 1880s were the heyday of the big philanthropic movements. Already in 1869 the Charity Organiza-tion Society had been formed to coordinate charitable giving, using the method of social casework to supervise donations and their uses (Woodroofe, 1963). The COS claimed a new scientific approach and pioneered training for social workers, alongside a rigorous doctrine of self-help which distinguished between the deserving and undeserving poor. Barnardo's methods were different: he was a pioneer in the art of pressure and the use of children as 'artistic fictions' in raising money. The children he rescued were re-dressed in rags and posed against depressing backgrounds. While no child was ever turned away, once rescued (and he used to go on 'philanthropic hunts' to find children) they were institutionalized or sent to the Dominions through his child emigration schemes (a way, he claimed, of removing the casual residuum) (Wagner, 1979, 1982).

Barnardo and the other big child welfare charities like the Church of England Children's Society (then the Waifs and Strays) saw children from the lower classes as social threats: the child in danger and the dangerous child were equally the ground from which crime, social disorder and vice grew. Platt (1977) has shown how the reformatory movement in the United States (like that in the UK, with which it was strongly connected) represented a response to the perceived evils of the city: the reformatory represented the countryside, morality, fresh air, instruction, order and character-building.

The NSPCC was to break the mould, picking up to some extent on the approach of the COS. Established as a national organization in 1889, it shifted from child rescue (placing children in institutions) to keeping children at home in order to attempt to reform their parents. The string of social legislation concerning the protection of children in Britain, France and the USA from the late nineteenth century was concerned with redrawing the relationship between parents and state, diminishing the authority of both parents, but especially of the father, and setting out the conditions under which the state's agents could enter the privacy of the home (Donzelot, 1980). Public housing, public health regulations, compulsory education – all these opened the family for inspection and began to delineate a set of parental duties.

While some (Donzelot, 1980; Meyer, 1983) have stressed this use of the child by the (French) state in its pedagogic invasion of the home to teach new norms, others have shown how reluctant, especially in England, were policy-makers to provide services, especially to women (for instance, maternity benefits and school meals – Lewis, 1980) for fear of undermining male responsibility. Moral reform, self-help and healthy motherhood, in so far as they did not undermine the responsibility of fatherhood, were the British blend of minimalism at the turn of the century. (The infant welfare movement will be discussed in the next chapter.) The NSPCC was able to strike the right balance in this context between the rights of the child to protection and the 'rights' of parents to behave as they wished in their own home. It avoided the poverty which the Independent Labour Party (ILP) and the Women's Cooperative Guild were revealing as factors in infant mortality and morbidity, and stressed that cruelty to children was a classless phenomenon. It began the shift of emphasis from the rights of parents to their duties, and established a system of state-regulated protection and supervision of parents who had failed. The Society did not prosecute large numbers of parents; rather, its work was to reform, and thus to exemplify the boundaries of parental roles and duties (Behlmer, 1982).

The success of the NSPCC was seen in legislation passed around the turn of the century. The Society had campaigned alongside the Social Purity Alliance and the National Vigilance Associations; all of them became skilled in parliamentary lobbying, the use of case histories and interviews to raise awareness through newspapers, and the exploitation of court cases and sensational stunts – like W.T. Stead's 'purchase' of a young virgin in 1885 to show the extent of the white slave trade. The resulting legislation included the 1872 Infant Life Protection Act; the 1885 Criminal Law Amendment Act (which raised the age of consent for girls from 13 to 16); the 1889 Prevention of Cruelty to Children Act; the 1908 Punishment of Incest Act; and the 1908 Children Act (which introduced juvenile courts).

These campaigns succeeded in their moral enterprise (Becker, 1963) in so far as they found an affinity with an anxiety amongst dominant and conservative groups about the family and responsibility as the basis of society (Platt, 1977). Yet these groups were very diverse, ranging from suffragettes, feminists, temperance groups, animal welfare groups, anti-vice groups, and religious groups of many different outlooks. Further, much of their work – as Jeffreys (1985) has shown – was radical and daring: for instance, the groups working with 'fallen women' uncovered and drew to a reluctant society's attention the common fact of child sexual abuse within the family, and the difficulties of getting evidence and therefore prosecutions. While, then, the overall effect of this pressure-group activity may have been to introduce a system of child protection based more on reforming the family than on liberating the child, this is not to say that the child's voice and rights were entirely neglected. A consequence for the child, however, was that he or she was cast, for the purpose of the campaigns, in a sentimental fashion, as innocent and vulnerable (for the knowing and sexually mature child is a threat, better dealt with by exclusion in prison or the new mental deficiency institutions). It is characteristic of child saving rather than child liberationist movements that the child is reduced to the adult's protection: in order to be worthy of public attention the child is infantilized, rendered innocent and without status (Ennew, 1986).

At the end of the nineteenth century the British state forged a new relationship with the family in order to meet the challenge of industrial and imperial competition from the USA, France and

Germany. The 1960s and 1970s were also to be an era when this relationship was recast, this time as a response to cultural change (the 'permissive society') and economic 'crisis' – the view that the post-war welfare state was expensive, outmoded and needed rethinking. At the same time unemployment and rising divorce levels have affected the lives of families and families' capacities to perform their tasks of social reproduction and caring, so we will now move on to the contemporary era to look at the meaning of anxiety about child abuse and its implications for childcare services for women and families.

The politics of child abuse: the NSPCC in the 1970s

It has been argued that child abuse has emerged as an issue because, as with other social problems, certain groups have had an interest in discovering and treating it (Pfohl, 1977). Nelson (1984) has argued that the 'discovery' of child abuse in the USA in the mid 1960s was contemporaneous with the growing women's rights movement and feminist campaigns in the fields of domestic violence to women, incest, rape and abortion. Child abuse, she argues, has been used as an apparently non-contentious issue to effect closure on these other issues and to construct abuse as a medico-social (or psychomedical) rather than a social-political problem. Parton (1985) has documented the moral panic and the interest groups and coalitions involved in the management of the response to the death of Maria Colwell in 1973, and connected these with a New Right concern with the 'crisis' in the family and an attack on the 'permissive society'. Neither argues that the abuse of children is not a serious and pervasive problem; rather that politicians, pressure groups, professions and the media shape and determine certain policy responses and close others, especially those to do with gender politics. It should be added that this process takes place at local as well as national level, as Campbell's (1988) account of the treatment of sexually abused children in Cleveland demonstrates.

Kempe, an American paediatrician, coined the term 'battered baby syndrome' in 1962, although the radiologist Coffey had called attention to unexplained bone injuries in children in 1946

(Pfohl, 1977). Kempe explained the 'syndrome' in terms of parental violence, perpetuated by sick (rather than criminal) individuals who were emotionally immature and childlike themselves. The NSPCC – at that time suffering from declining referrals – imported Kempe's model into England, aided by paediatricians, whose specialism was also suffering (because of improved infant health). Shifting from 'cruelty' work on the one hand, and from disease work on the other, into this new area of behavioural work offered both groups a new clientele.

In the decade following Kempe's article there was an enormous growth of interest in the 'syndrome' in the American paediatric and psychiatric journals, and in the general media (Nelson, 1984). The NSPCC was therefore able to import ready-made expertise, and in 1968 established its Battered Child Research Unit in London to raise awareness of the issue,

> encouraged by friends of the Society in America and with the support of leading paediatricians in Britain . . . which, in the words of the Director, was intended to 'strive to create an informed body of opinion about the battered child syndrome and to devise methods of treatment'. (Baher *et al.*, 1976)

The NSPCC gained influence at the DHSS when its former director, Joan Court, joined its Social Work Service: the interest of A.W. Franklin, a paediatrician, brought it into a powerful position. In early 1973 Franklin organized a conference on child abuse and neglect at Tunbridge Wells, attended by Sir Keith Joseph and senior DHSS civil servants, after which the Inquiry into the death of Maria Colwell was announced. This was the first of a series of public inquiries into the deaths of children, supervised by social workers, at their parents' or step-parents' hands, all of which have continued to rouse intense media interest in the efficacy of social workers in child protection work. Franklin established BASPCAN (the British Association for the Study and Prevention of Child Abuse and Neglect), and he and his medical and NSPCC colleagues used a tone of authority in shaping the discussion and policies on child protection. In her obituary on Franklin, Cooper, another prominent paediatrician in this field, said:

> As knowledge about maltreated children grew during the 1960s and 1970s, and the extent of the problem began to be

realized by a growing number of professionals, his inspired leadership brought together experts in many fields. With the idea of these individuals sharing knowledge and skills, the Tunbridge Wells Study Group was born in 1973 under his Chairmanship. It caught the interest and attention of Sir Keith Joseph, then Secretary of State for Social Services. As a result the short report of the meeting and the final resolutions were published by the DHSS and in the *British Medical Journal*, receving wide publicity. The resolutions stressed the need for interdisciplinary collaboration to study and help abused children and their families. The involvement of lawyers and the need for legal controls were highlighted . . . . This was the time of the Maria Colwell Enquiry and Dr Franklin was the paediatrician whose wisdom greatly assisted the Committee's difficult task of understanding all the issues. (Cooper, 1984 : 16)

The NSPCC had adapted Kempe's medical, clinic-based system to a community-based social work organization. Its Research Unit's first director had been Joan Court, whose views on child abuse stressed abnormalities and deprivations in battering parents' own childhoods, separations and poor relationships with parents. She viewed child abuse as transmitted through generations, a 'sample of the cycle of deprivation' (Court, 1974; DHSS, 1974: 17). The research team, using an action-research approach, then opened a therapeutic day nursery in 1971 – the Denver House Day Nursery, which put into practice Kempe's dictum that child abuse requires parental therapy:

It should be stressed, as this study makes clear from the outset, that when one intervenes in the process of child abuse or the 'failure to thrive' syndrome one is not acting on behalf of the child against the parents, but rather for the abusive parents as well . . . child abusers are, themselves, in very deep pain; and by their rescue one does not only protect the child and other children to come, one often strengthens a marriage and, when things go well, one ends up either with an intact family very much improved, or with the understanding . . . that an effort must be made to find permanently other arrangements through termination of parental rights or adoptions. (Kempe, preface to Baher, *et al.* 1976: ix)

In 1968 the NSPCC had also formed therapeutic playgroups, which were clearly distinguished from those other NSPCC playgroups that were open to any children in their socially deprived areas. These therapeutic playgroups were to accept only children referred by NSPCC or other social workers, or by GPS or health visitors (Rose, 1973). One problem for such specialized services is finding sufficient numbers of cases, and the therapeutic day nursery staff experienced lulls in referrals of battered children and their siblings:

> Consequently we had been persuaded to take on several cases in which the children had no current injury on referral but whose mothers had admitted handling them roughly in the past and expressed a continual fear of injuring them again. (Baher *et al.*, 1976: 4–5)

Parton has argued that the NSPCC discovered and promoted the idea of the battered child predominantly because its survival was at stake. By 1964 only 9,632 of the 120,000 children helped by the NSPCC had been physically assaulted. Neglect and emotional problems were an area of work in which the NSPCC increasingly competed with the growing (and more professionalized) local authority social-work services, especially after the 1971 creation of social services departments. The Society sought ways of abandoning the limitations of the old concern with 'cruelty', and widened its work to what was now seen as a medico-social problem, needing less supervision and legal intervention than psychotherapeutic or behavioural treatment. It set out to 'educate' the medical, social-work and legal professions – partly by the use of research studies from its own Research Unit, and by using Kempe's expertise to legitimate their authority to comment on child abuse scandals and to influence thinking in the media and amongst civil servants in the DHSS.

The NSPCC was successful in its new role in so far as by 1984 it had thirteen Special Units which were responsible for child protection work in certain areas, and for maintaining the Child Abuse Registers. It provided training in its methods of investigation and treatment, and a specialized casework service. Some Units had day centres attached, and in addition the Society expanded to sixty-five playgroups and four daycare centres. These daycare centres, unlike the playgroups, are designed to involve the whole family:

> Each of these facilities are 'therapeutic' in that they set out to tackle directly some of the damaging effects upon children

of abuse, deprivation or family problems, while also trying to promote the child's development and social integration. Day centres focus on the whole family and are thus able to engage in skilled Treatment Programmes which are geared to the particular circumstances and needs of the child and his or her family. (NSPCC 1984 Centenary Background Notes – publicity material)

In the early 1980s the NSPCC opened family centres, such as the Basildon Family Treatment Centre and the Farnborough Family Craft Centre. Like other organizations' centres they are diverse, but portrayed to those who support the NSPCC as a charity in reassuringly firm, paternalist, tones:

The family centres . . . provide an actual place were [sic] mothers, fathers and children can be together but away from the stresses of their normal lives. . . . The atmosphere is almost that of a social club. There are mothers sitting around discussing the fashions in mail order catalogues, children playing amicably together only a few feet away . . . . [The officer in charge says] The mothers themselves are like children . . . [The] social worker with the Unit describes the work of the family centre as being to 'provide a kind of extended family – a very warm caring atmosphere. If you get some mother who's very damaged there's nothing you can do about that. You fill in the gaps left by their own parents, show the mothers you care about them. You try to modify the child's behaviour so that the mother can cope – and modify the mother's behaviour so that the child can cope. We give them the love and suport they've never had in their lives.' (Rafferty: 'Where can a battered child find safety?', *Children's Friend*, Autumn 1984: 5)

The NSPCC has moved away from direct 'cruelty' work to promote skills in assessment and treatment of physically, emo-tionally and sexually abused children. Like all the voluntary agencies, however, it has not been able to expand indefinitely, and continuing government restrictions on expenditure have limited the grants it has received from social services departments for its child protection work, to the extent that in 1990 it had to review its work, and decided to contract somewhat (its income in 1990 was around £26m) (*Community Care*, 18 October 1990). The NSPCC, then, like other voluntary organizations, has been, since the 1960s, both modernizing and attempting to control its work, vulnerable to political change and cutbacks. The *ideological* impact has been more important: the interest in developing more welfare pluralism, its part in the discourse on the 'crisis in the family', and the overshadowing of the issue of violence against women in the family by the narrow focus on child abuse.

While child abuse was a strong theme in social-political discourse in the 1970s (as it continues to be), so too was the question of the provision for the child in Care. Both issues have culminated in the 1989 Children Act, to which I shall return after looking at criticisms which have been made of the system of public Care for children. The consequence of highlighting child *abuse* is that debate on children's *needs* is handled in pathologized terms: rather than the social and psychological benefits of daycare and other children's services, the focus is on the treatment of parents.

The Care system, daycare and prevention in the 1970s and 1980s

Why, before the 1991 implementation of the Children Act, is 'prevention' of entry to Care taken to be self-evidently a good thing in the family centre and local authority documents studied for the research? The attitudes underlying this assumption have included those I mentioned at the beginning of this chapter: the liberationist/libertarian view of the 1960s and 1970s, with both a right- and a left-wing version, that sought to protect working-class families from the state's invasion (left-wing) and asserted that families should not be 'nannied' by social workers (right-wing). In between were more centrist views which pointed to the over-representation in Care of black children (e.g. Ahmed, 1987; Cheetham, 1981) and children of one-parent and poor families (Holman, 1976), and to the failure of the Care system and its social workers to promote the educational (Jackson, 1983) or psychological (Rowe and Lambert, 1973) development of children. The 1989 Act and family centres blend neo-traditionalist views on parental responsibility and family privacy, while incorporating left/critical views on the shortcomings of the Care system. The upshot is that the Act and family centres seek to divert children and families from the Care system (by treating parents) rather than to improve the Care system and the range of childcare services, such as day and residential care.

As I showed in Chapter 1, prevention is now associated with self-help and self-responsibility in health and welfare, and this twist in its meaning can give professionals greater control over their clients, as well as increasing their gatekeeping role in restricting or regulating access to (scarce) services. As we noted in Chapter 2, social services strategy documents and family centre documents have presented prevention as a progressive avoidance of the damaging consequences of being in Care. Being in Care has been equated with emotional deprivation and stigma, partly because many of the 'dependent' clients of social services have been identified as people who themselves grew up in Care. Packman talks of the 'rule of pessimism' amongst social workers; in her sample:

> Fairly frequent reference was also made to the damaging consequences of 'care', which had to be borne in mind when reaching decisions. There were anxieties about institut-ionalisation, the alienation of children from their families and the tendency for them to languish in care for long periods. (in Packman *et al.*, 1986: 106)

Criticisms of social workers' effectiveness in planning for children in Care and in protecting children at risk of abuse continued during the 1980s. A DHSS report entitled *Social Work Decision-Making in Child Care* (1985) provided an overview of nine major research studies involving 2,000 children, and concluded that 'the scene portrayed is generally quite disturbing and depressing'. The report found that decisions tended to be made rapidly and often in crisis, so that admissions to Care were often not well planned; less attention was given to what was to happen after admission than to whether or not to admit; social-work attention faded, and discharge or remaining in Care was often not the result of social-work planing. The report noted that parents who requested Care were offered few alternatives and were 'put through the hoops'.

As well as negative attitudes to Care and lack of commitment to working positively with children in Care, social workers have tended to hold poor views of local authority daycare services; they have done little to improve them or to make them more available, or to work to keep strong links between the services, their users, and their families and networks (Kerslake and Cramp, 1988; Tunstill, 1985). Local authority day nurseries were viewed negatively by the family centre workers and social workers I interviewed; they were seen as causing problems because of the separation of mother and young child. The conclusion was not that daycare could be improved but that the service should be replaced by one more focused on parents. The London Borough of Camden, for example, had already moved in that direction in 1974 (Marshall, 1982; Urwin, 1974). As one of their managers put it:

> The wider social services departments offer group experiences and day care for the mentally disordered, the elderly, the physically handicapped and the disadvantaged child. Now they can extend this type of intervention to offer the disadvantaged parent a new supportive experience *with* the child, instead of encouraging the parent to *leave* the child ostensibly to promote his welfare. (Brill, 1976: 52)

The supportive experience would promote the mother's mental health by preventing depression and isolation, and would not weaken the emotional well-being of the child by separation. Research – as I shall discuss in Chapter 6 – shows that it is not the separation of mother and child in daycare that can cause problems, but the *qualities* of the care that are at issue. By the late 1970s, however, local authority nurseries were seen as outmoded, as no longer relevant, and their transformation into family centres began.

While most local authorities in my study shared a negative view of day nurseries, there were some London boroughs with Labour-controlled councils which promoted a service and social benefit model of daycare: instead of attempting to reduce dependence on social services by therapeutic or behavioural means, they offered daycare as a benefit to the child and as an opportunity for the parent(s) to work or study, and thus gain independence and some control over their lives (Dennis and Wallis, 1982). Government restrictions on local authorities' expenditure, however, have limited what might have been achieved.

'Prevention', then, has covered a range of diverse aims, but in the 1980s there was a lack of clarity amongst local authorities about how such a term might be made operational (Tunstill, 1985). Because of negative images of Care, success has tended to be measured in terms of a fall in the numbers of children entering Care. This index was one taken by the House of Commons Select Committee on *Children in Care* (The Short Report, 1984), which gave official recognition to the gathering consensus that too many (deprived) children were entering the Care system during the 1970s.

The statistics show an increase in numbers of children in Care from 1973, apparently reflecting more intervention by social workers worried by criticisms made during the Maria Colwell Inquiry. Numbers in Care continued to rise until 1977, after which they declined rapidly. A close look at the statistics does not support the view that social workers were taking more and more children into Care. The rise in numbers in the early 1970s was a result of the fact that the 1969 Children and Young Persons Act now included in the Care statistics children who were formerly shown in the criminal statistics (Dingwall and Eekelaar, 1984). While the peak for numbers in Care and admissions to Care was reached in 1977, these numbers of children must be compared with the general child population (which was declining); and from the ratio thus arrived at it can be seen that the increase through the 1970s was small, peaking in 1980 with 7.7 children per 1,000 in Care. For under-5s the increase was remarkably small, and the ratio peaked at 3.9 per 1,000 in 1976. What increases there have been are therefore accounted for by two factors: first, an increasing proportion of older delinquent children included in the Care statistics; second, caution about discharging children once they are in Care. Fewer children came into Care over the period, but those who did tended to remain there for a long time, reflecting a second trend in child welfare: planning for permanence, a trend consolidated by the 1975 Children Act, which made it easier for children in Care to be freed for adoption. Related to this are the facts that children have been the subjects of more court orders when received into Care, that fewer came 'voluntarily' into Care with parental consent (The Short Report, 1984), and that of those who did, many tended to drift: to settle into Care rather than be rehabilitated to their families.

There are two opposing trends, then, in child welfare policy and practice: prevention and compulsion; family participation and rights, and loss of parental authority (Packman *et al.*, 1986). There was no evidence of widespread coercive child removal practices in the late 1970s and early 1980s (Dingwall and Eekelaar, 1984), but there may have been an intensification of control for a small proportion of families who had lost their parental authority. At the same time, there has been a change in the use of services such as day nurseries from simply giving parents a break (respite) to monitoring and treatment of those on the brink of the Care system (those now 'in need').

Keeping chidren with their families or working with parents' consent, an idea originating with the NSPCC in the 1880s, has been an aim of policies dating from the 1948 Children Act:

> To keep the family together must be the first aim, and the separation of a child from its parents can only be justified when there is no possibility of securing adequate care for a child in his own home. (Home Office, 1948: para. 19)

In 1960 the Committee on Children and Young Persons, chaired by Lord Ingleby, reported. It too stressed preventive, family-focused policies in keeping children out of Care and preventing delinquency. The Seebohm Report (1968), which was to lead to the establishment of large social services departments with more professionalized social workers, stressed an integrated family service, locally accessible provision and social workers developing resources in the community. It envisaged such work in the context of general preventive services: better housing, health promotion, adequate incomes, full employment, and a well-developed and imaginative education system. It also included under-5s' services which, of course, have never been universally available in the UK (paras 427–54). Social workers were to do specific preventive work either with individuals and families 'at risk of developing problems through personal, environmental, life-cycle or life-event circumstances', or with 'people who are already in distress and who need services to reduce the severity of the problem and to prevent it deteriorating'.

In 1975 the National Children's Bureau (which has strongly influenced DHSS policy – see Chapter 4) set up a working party, chaired by Professor Roy Parker, to consider the needs of children separated from their families (Parker, 1980). This working party included, from the childcare establishment, Mia

Kellmer Pringle, Director of the National Children's Bureau, and Jane Rowe, who had produced the report *Children Who Wait* (Rowe and Lambert, 1973). A more critical member was Robert Holman, then a Professor of Social Administration and author of the Child Poverty Action Group Report (1976) on *Inequality in Childcare*, who subsequently (as shown in Chapter 2) developed thinking in the more participative family centres. This group originated in criticisms of the quality of residential care for children and of social workers' effectiveness in planning for and protecting them. While the committee agreed that more resources should be going to young children, they nevertheless took 'account of political realities' and decided not to aim too high (Parker, 1980: 7–8). They therefore placed the emphasis on prevention, which they defined as strengthening the family. Preventing children coming into Care is a major aim, because Care produces damaged adults. Daycare was not seen as a social benefit in its own right, and its primary task was enlarged from providing a service directly to children to assisting 'parents in their task of child care'. The committee recommended that parents be involved in daycare, for this would teach the skills of parenting and build up confidence. While the report acknowledged the role of poverty in family breakdown, prevention was discussed in terms of preparation for parenthood classes, marital social work, sympathetic support from social workers and health visitors, group care for depressed mothers and their children, daycare for children which involved mothers, and a new philosophy – shared care – which would underpin the 1989 Children Act.

Shared care and disabled children

In childhood disability we find an example of an area where the state (grudgingly) shares (or at least acknowledges the principle of) care with parents: in this area parents are seen as deserving of state aid. They are thus less likely to find their autonomy threatened by consumption of state services: there is no blemish on their character, for their need is fortuitous. Yet the idea of shared care has been generalized from the field of child disability to that of children in need – which includes children from families where there is poor care or abuse. Shared care of disabled children developed between hospital and parents, and the National Children's Bureau connected the idea of shared care of handicapped children in health settings with that of deprived children in day nurseries, or indeed in Care.

In the field of care for mentally handicapped (as they were then known) children, great changes took place during the 1970s. From 1971 children were no longer to be placed in long-stay segregated institutions; instead they would be cared for in partnership with community-based, social care services (DHSS, 1971). This was partly a result of parent pressure and partly a result of several scandals over conditions in long-stay hospitals (Shearer, 1981). Doctors in this field had to shift towards a greater partnership with parents or risk seeing their specialism discredited and shifted to other professions.

In the early 1970s the Hester Adrian Research Centre in Manchester began teaching parents of mentally handicapped children principles and techniques in observation and assessment, and in the achievement of specific tasks. This became known as the Parental Involvement Project, and in giving parents the skills to teach and monitor their children, the Centre noted marked improvements in children's functioning and in their IQs. Other workers were developing the same approach, notably John and Elizabeth Newson in Nottingham, and Dr F.S.W. Brimble-combe, a paediatrician, at Honeylands in Exeter. Brimblecombe (1976) wrote an article in the DHSS journal *Social Work Service* asking 'How about parents as partners?'. He described his Family Support Unit, which offered short-term residential respite care on demand for disabled children and led to the Home Intervention Project whereby therapists visited families to assist them in their children's development. The whole family attended six-monthly meetings, and to the staff's surprise demand for respite care did not rise: clearly the parents were willing to care for their own children as long as they had support services which they could decide how to use.

Other projects followed – some, such as Kith and Kids in London, set up by parents' groups. Government approval, and the dissemination of the approach, were provided by the National Children's Bureau conference in 1981 on 'Partnership in the Care of Children with Special Needs'. The conference echoed the spirit of the Court Report on *Child Health Services* (1976), which had also advocated the involvement of parents of disabled children in their treatment, care and assessment. Further impetus to the parents' movement was given by the Warnock Report on *Special Educational Needs* (1978), which stressed the integration of children into ordinary schools, and the normal rights of parents in relation to their children's health and education.

Parker's committee would in 1975 anticipate these developments, and indeed make legitimate their emerging framework of shared care. But the committee were using the idea in relation to parents on the brink between responsibility and loss of parental rights:

> 'Shared care' might mean a number of things. It may mean encouraging mutual help between families; it may mean day care or partial residential care, either regularly or at certain points of crisis. It may mean that certain caring tasks are shared with others . . . families who most need help may be reluctant to share care. . . . 'Shared care' may provide the link between prevention, substitute care and rehabilitation. We believe it is the actual tasks of daily caring which need to be shared more than they are. (Parker (ed.), 1980: 135)

Conclusion: the 1989 Children Act

The Parker committee's reworking of 'prevention' established the rationale for a parent-orientated system of childcare provision; it combined the radical libertarianism and community work of Holman with the respectable psychomedicalism of Kellmer Pringle. It was the collective (yet internally differentiated) voice of the childcare establishment, those powerful in this area of social work, able to shape the discourse on child welfare and the needs of children. The Parker Committee, the DHSS/DES conference on Low Cost Day Provision for the Under-Fives (1976) and the Short Committee on *Children in Care* (1984) were settings in which the childcare establishment could shape and frame policy and, as in their responses to the child abuse inquiries, handle criticisms of social work's effectiveness and goals by providing a politically and professionally acceptable way forward.

The 1989 Children Act unified family and childcare law, and meshed family support with child protection rather than opposing them. It replaces all previous children's legislation, and incorporates many of the research findings and principles I have discussed in this chapter. The Act had cross-party support so that, like family centres, it can be seen to reflect both a degree of consensus and the mix of attitudes that have shaped social policy and social work with children over the last two decades. It takes the welfare of the child as paramount, but at the same time it protects the family from intervention, which is sanctioned by the courts only when it can be shown that such a course is better than not intervening. Parental responsiblity is a strong theme, and such responsibility is seen to rest in duties, not rights. Most parents are assumed to exercise their responsibilities to the child's advantage; where they do not, then responsibility can be transferred to another person such as a relative, or to the local authority if the child is in Care.

The Act attempts to prevent 'drift' in Care. 'Voluntary' Care is abolished; instead, local authorities must provide 'accommodation' where children will be 'looked after', possibly on the model of respite care for disabled children. This should be less of a conveyor belt to Care orders from the courts because parents must be involved in plans and arrangements, and their responsibilities will not easily be surrendered, though they may be shared with the local authority.

Local authorities must also provide a range of preventive services including family centres to support families with children in need, to promote the care of children within their own families, and to reduce the need for recourse to the courts for Care proceedings. Children in need are defined as those whose development or standard of health would be impaired without the provision of such services, and disabled children. Services are to be provided where possible in partnership with voluntary, private or other statutory agencies. Partnership with parents is the key principle, on the assumption that it is the duty of the local authority to promote children's upbringing by their own family. When children are the subject of Care orders, there is tighter judicial supervision of the grounds and purpose of Care, as well as complaints procedures and mechanisms for involving parents as consumers rather than clients. The Act makes social workers more accountable both to courts and to parents, and seeks to give children a voice: local authorities must take account of the wishes of the child, and of their cultural, religious and linguistic background.

As we have seen in this chapter, and as we will see in the next, the Act incorporates two poles of libertarian thinking. From the Right, the neo-traditional notion of family privacy – 'normal' families should not need public services – and from the Left, a concern to empower poor families and parents in conflict with the state. Both incorporate a certain mistrust of professionals, and see accountability to the courts and to parents as the mechanism of controlling such power. The Act provides the framework for positive and progressive family and childcare services: at the time of writing, however, it appeared that government restrictions on expenditure would narrow its scope and reintroduce stigma and bureaucracy to family support services by rationing them to the most desperate and deviant (Packman and Jordan, 1991; Tunstill, 1991). Diversion from the Care system would continue to be a form of neglect in the community, forcing many families, not assessed as 'in need', to cope without services.

We will return to these issues in Chapters 6 and 7. Now we turn to the idea of parental responsibility, to uncover the discourse underlying this concept. We have shown that parental participation has different meanings which depend on the reason for parents' involvement with care services. Working parents who pay for places in nurseries, parents who are active in their children's schooling, parents of disabled children, can participate in state services and their running with no aspersions on their character or reduction in their autonomy. Where care of children is at issue, parents' status is reduced; their rights and those of their children may be (properly) opposed. The next chapter will deepen our look at the way families, and especially mothers, are involved in the system of childcare in the UK: we will return to the daycare services as such in the final chapter.

CHAPTER 4

ROOTS OF FAMILY CENTRES
Motherhood and the state

This chapter will argue that social policies in Britain are constructed around anxiety about family fragility and change. It will be concerned with debates on delinquency and child abuse which have viewed these social problems as transmitted or influenced by pathologies in family life, and by deviant family forms – especially female headed families, and especially those dependent on state welfare. The chapter will look at the historical roots of current neo-traditionalist family policies. It will look at the public debates on family life, at the politicians, professions and voluntary organizations who have been powerful in shaping perceptions of social problems, and at how gender images of 'good mothers' as responsible and vigilant have been created. The boundary between the family and the state is one that is always fluid, but I shall argue that since the early 1970s there has been a strong attempt to push care back on to women in families. Family services such as pre-school playgroups and Home-Start will be discussed as examples of the shifting of responsibility for childcare back from the state on to women. Women's own needs for assistance with caring tasks as well as for protection and assistance if they are abused have been marginalized in the discourses on child abuse and the fragility of the family.

Maternal education in the early twentieth century

The family is an institution which is in constant interaction with the state, and its form is affected by the demands made upon it and the resources given it by society. The state, through its spectrum of policies – housing and architecture, leisure, employment, income policies, transport – shapes the environment and social network of family life. While there are undoubtedly changes in family structures (as there always have been – there is no golden age of 'the' nuclear or extended family [Anderson, 1971]), the family interacts with its environment and has different demands placed upon it in different eras, classes, societies. Such demands are profoundly gendered, which means that we cannot conceive of the family as a single unit, but as one composed of members who experience the demands society makes of it in different ways (Land, 1989).

As we discussed in Chapter 3, over this century all Western societies have seen the development of the expectation that mothers would undertake more intensive socialization of children, taking responsibility not just for their physical health but for their emotional and intellectual development. Norms of childcare (the importance of play, of talk, of attention and warmth) have been promoted by the medical profession, the emerging social-work profession, community nurses and health visitors, and schools (Badinter, 1981; Bernstein, 1975; Donzelot, 1980; Lewis, 1980). Within this broad remit, methods of childcare have swung from the permissive to the disciplinarian in response to changing industrial, political and social conditions (Ehrenreich and English, 1976), but the changes in child-rearing styles have both given a task to and grown from the existence of childcare experts. The assumption that the working-class family is fragile and at risk of not performing its socializing tasks satisfactorily has sanctioned a degree of ideological manipulation and intrusion into the 'privacy' of the family which is otherwise unacceptable in Britain.

'Proper' families are in part promoted by the state through fiscal, housing and other social policies. Deviant families – and this usually means families headed by women, or families where the man is not in work – can lose their autonomy and fall under welfare supervision. Gordon's (1988) work on child protection agencies in Boston earlier in the century showed the challenge which female-headed families posed to social workers and the state: giving material aid or pensions seemed to undermine the traditional power and authority relations in families. Anxiety about female-headed families reflects conservative fears about the growing autonomy of women and children and the corresponding decline of male authority. Social workers' help, which partly empowered and helped poor women, also controlled them, lest it threaten the norm of male authority over and domination of the family.

At the turn of the century Britain faced growing industrial competition from Germany, the USA and Japan. Although the birth rate was high, so too was infant mortality and morbidity, resulting in difficulties in raising a fit army to fight the Boer War. This revelation led to the 1904 *Report of the Committee on Physical Deterioration*, which argued that deterioration was a matter not just of living standards or industry, but of childhood (Lewis, 1980). It recommended the creation of the School Medical Service to screen and treat impairment. Rising concern at the quality of the population produced the infant welfare movement, led by Medical Officers of Health (MOHS). The MOHS, voluntary and charity organizations, and local authorities set up clinics for mothers and infants: by 1916 there were 160 branches of voluntary organizations and 35 local authorities with infant welfare clinics, which increased during the First World War. As Lewis (1980) has demonstrated, the scope of these clinics remained limited to education of or advice to mothers, on the assumption that it was working-class ignorance which was to blame for infant deaths. The avoidance of the issue of poverty (though there were a few exceptions, such as the Women's Labour League clinics) and failure to provide medical treatment or material help to mothers for fear of undermining fathers' responsibilities meant that these public health clinics remained essentially conservative.

The MOHS, the Fabians, and the birth control movement were all, during the first third of the century, influenced to some extent by Social Darwinism and the eugenics movement (Davin, 1978). Their views differed somewhat on how far prevention of 'inefficiency' was possible, and on whether the sickly were inherently so or had become so through poor diet, rearing or environment. While some of the more extreme eugenists had advocated a 'weeding-out' process and a 'better dead' approach, by the 1920s and 1930s the dramatically falling birth rate meant that the focus shifted to the quality of life, given its relative scarcity after the First World War.

Preparation for parenthood was an essential part of the Peckham Experiment with its Pioneer Health Centre, originally established in 1926. In many ways it was ahead of its time with its view that individual well-being is linked to social life: the biologists Pearse and Crocker took the family as the unit of observation. Despite the fact that the broadly healthy working class was selected for membership of the centre and those 'from the stagnant verges' of society were avoided (Pearse and Crocker, 1943: 42), 90 per cent of the members were found to have something wrong with them. Unlike the *laissez-faire* eugenists, Pearse and Crocker were interventionist biologists who wished to till the 'familial soil'. The Centre, with its sports and social activities, was also designed to provide for courting by local young people, ensuring that narrow social circles did not undermine adequate natural selection, for 'inbreeding is fraught with peril to racial vitality' (*ibid*.: 277). Positive health before marriage and wanted pregnancies were their aims:

> Here then in the Centre is a situation in which the 'practice' of Health in its positive cultural aspect becomes for the first time possible: – family culture on a rational basis, beginning with the enrichment of the soil before marriage. (*ibid*.: 246)

In health and welfare practice, then, from the early twentieth century we find an attention to the norms of family life which emphasizes the couple: the mother caring and domestic, the father the wage-earner and the source of authority.

Delinquency: from family casework to parental responsibility

In the post-war era delinquency has been framed as a family (rather than class or genetic, for instance) problem, and under the social democratic consensus from the mid 1940s to the early 1970s social-work services were developed to control, supervise, and prevent delinquency. This focus on the family is one side of the broader cult of domesticity which accompanied women's return to the home after the war, and of the assumptions of 'normal' family life which were built into the welfare state. By the social democratic view I mean not only post-war Labour Party politicians but the Fabian and liberal academics and professionals in the welfare field who have influenced politics and contributed to policy. D.J. West's work at Cambridge is a prime example of this sociopsychological perspective in criminology. Despite criticism from radical sociology, this perspective has been able to stay afloat through DHSS and Home Office funding, though under Conservatism during the 1980s it also suffered alongside the more critical wings of social science.

During the 1950s and 1960s a clear line of work appeared, focusing on youth, the family and community. This research, typified by Mays' or Willmott's work, asked why delinquency should continue in the era of post-war 'affluence' and the welfare state. Subcultural explanations, reflecting contemporary American sociology, appeared too broad to indicate precise means of intervention, so that the delinquent was now investigated in his or her family, using positivist measures and psychoanalytic concepts. Parker and Giller (1981) cite Wilson and Herbert (1978), West and Farrington (1971) and Wadsworth (1979) as researchers who received government funding and coopted the insights of the labelling perspective to enhance their positivist approaches. It is this type of research – 'relevant', relatively uncritical, with clear recommendations – which the Social Science Research Council (SSRC; now the Economic and Social Research Council), Home Office Research Unit and DHSS have preferred. Local government reorganization and the amalgamation of social-work services into social services departments in the early 1970s meant upheavals in the DHSS and the Home Office, and Parker and Giller suggest that, in the circumstances, the Departments simply initiated more of the same kind of research, more childcare studies, often tied to the childcare establishment – the National Children's Bureau, the Thomas Coram Institute, and the Dartington Research Unit.

In the fields of delinquency and child abuse, then, parental and home circumstances have been heavily researched. West's was a longitudinal study of 411 boys, followed from the age of 8 into youth and adulthood. His conclusion has consistently been that the boys who were destined to become delinquent had less fortunate backgrounds than those who were not, and that low family income, large family size, parental criminality, low intelligence and poor parental behaviour and child-rearing were associated with delinquency (West and Farrington, 1973). When his cohort had attained adulthood, West wrote:

> The typical criminogenic family is beset by chronic problems. The Cambridge Study found no evidence for the predominant importance of the circumstances of early life over those of later years. Delinquents tend to come from families with continuing disturbances that affected children in their school days as much as in their infancy and which manifested themselves in many different ways. For instance, parents who let their children spend most of their leisure time away from the family, fathers who never took part in their son's leisure activities, and mothers whose expectations for their son's future career prospects were low in comparison with his educational achievement level, were all more likely than others to have sons becoming delinquent. (West, 1982: 56–7)

Wadsworth's (1979) research, which used the National Child Development Survey, also stressed family life as the key variable in the genesis of delinquency. While he too was critical of the 'early disruption' explanation for delinquency and disturbance, his finding was that family circumstances – disruption of parent-child relationship in early life, through parental death, divorce or separation – were associated with later delinquency. Marital breakdown and illegitimate pregnancies were also associated with the early disruption groups, though only a minority of 'early disrupters' are accounted for by all these measures. He concluded that while early disruption may produce a *risk* of becoming delinquent, it is other factors to do with circumstances at the time of the offence which need researching – situational and opportunity factors.

One situational factor which has been researched, and was incorporated into Conservative crime policies of the 1980s, is another family variable: parental vigilance. Wilson worked with Herbert (1978) on Home Office-commissioned research on families known to social services departments, and the development of their children. This study showed that parents in poor neighbourhoods occasionally took measures to protect their children from the 'bad' environment and, while reducing their scope for play and friendships, did succeed in preventing delinquency. In subsequent research (Wilson, 1980), also sponsored by the Home Office, she showed that some parents, in contrast to the strict parents, were excessively lax in their supervision and care, a quality associated with deprivation or 'social handicap'. She argued, as did West (1982), that parental supervision or chaperonage – and, conversely, the lack of it – is a key variable in the development or prevention of delinquency, as close supervision overcomes the effects of 'social handicap'. Thus, she suggested, parents could be helped to prevent delinquency by improving the quality of their relationships with their children, being realistic about delinquency, closely monitoring their children's choice of friends, and spending more time with them. She was cautious about the implications of her findings, arguing that lax parenting methods are an unfortunate generalization of middle-class permissive methods of child-rearing, and secondly that lax methods in the negative sense:

> are often the result of chronic stress situations arising from frequent or prolonged spells of unemployment, physical or mental disabilities amongst members of the family, and an often permanent condition of poverty. If these factors are ignored and parental laxness is seen instead as an 'attitude' which can be shifted by education or by punitive measures, then our findings are being misinterpreted. It is the position of the most disadvantaged groups in society, and not the individual, which needs improvement in the first place. (Wilson, 1980: 233–4)

Here she warned of the policy shift which was to come under the Conservatives, when parental education and responsibility, already themes in Labour Party policies, would assume a harder and more punitive form. Labour Party policies and the research they were based on emphasized the family as a key variable in the treatment and prevention of delinquency, but proposed a soft form of social-work support for problem families based on a family service. Many who argued for a unified family casework service when the Seebohm Committee was looking at local authority personal social services in the mid 1960s were members of the Labour Party.

The party had taken up the issue of the rising crime rate and juvenile crime in the 1964 general election (Hall, 1976). Lord

Longford's report *Crime: A challenge to us all* (1964) had reasserted the link between delinquency and deprivation, but saw social and individual inadequacy, not poverty, as a cause of maladjustment. His report reaffirmed the view that the family must accept its responsibility for control, socialization and the transmission of common cultural values. The family had been weakened by affluence, individualism and the 'get-rich-quick' ethos of the affluent society: 'For acquisitiveness as the overriding motive in life, socialists substitute the ideas of mutual service and work towards a society in which everyone has a chance to play a full and responsible part' (Longford, 1964: 5). Longford commended West's work, and echoed his recommendations for preventing delinquency: general support services such as home helps, crèches, training for early school leavers, as well as social casework for incompetent parents and parent education in schools.

The Labour Party social work approach was underlined in the White Paper *The Child, the Family and the Young Offender* (Home Office, 1965) and a shift to a welfare model of juvenile delinquency began, though it was never completed owing to pressure from magistrates and civil libertarians (see Pitts [1988] for a full account of the politics of juvenile justice). The creation of the large social services departments in 1971 expanded the scope and resources of social workers who now dealt with delinquents on Care orders.

The Labour Party, then, had introduced a model of delinquency control and treatment based on social work with families; delinquency arose in the nexus of deprivation and poor parenting: 'affluence' and individualism in families were as much to blame as poverty. In this respect there seemed to be little disagreement between Labour and the Conservative administration of 1970–74: both shared a view of disadvantage and deviance as transmitted through families, and parenthood was the point at which what Sir Keith Joseph would call the 'cycle of deprivation' (see below) could be broken. The politics of juvenile justice under subsequent Conservative administrations, however, reveals a qualitative shift in the view of parental behaviour: responsibility became the key word, as it did in health care, in housing and schooling, and sanctions such as fining parents would be proposed rather than social-work help.

The Conservatives under Margaret Thatcher sought not so much to support the family as to preserve it by protecting it from the welfare state and its professionals, who were seen as weakening families by undermining their independence (Fitzgerald, 1983). Conservative policies have asserted parental responsibility as a strategy for preserving marriage, and gender and power relations, in their traditional forms. In juvenile justice, holding parents responsible for their children's misdemeanours has been stressed (Tutt, 1981). In the 1980 White Paper *Young Offenders* it was stated:

> the Government believes it is important that the courts should . . . be able more effectively to bring home to parents their responsibilities in relation to juveniles who offend. There are clearly cases in which it is quite wrong that their children commit criminal offences . . . the Government will substantially strengthen, simplify and clarify the present provision under which parents can be involved in the consequences of their children offending (Home Office, 1980: para. 53)

The proposal to make parents pay fines for 14–16-year-olds 'will encourage the courts to assert the duty of parents to act responsibly towards their children and take all steps within their power to prevent them committing criminal offences' (para. 54). The Conservatives, then, have tried to distance themselves from Labour's family support approach, though their preventive provision remained similar, albeit more tightly targeted and with more emphasis on volunteers, preparation for parenthood, involvement of mothers in playgroups, and home visiting schemes.

The 'cycle of deprivation' and the parental role

Sir Keith Joseph, while he was Secretary of State for Social Services, coined the term 'cycle of deprivation' in his speech to the Pre-School Playgroups Association in 1972. He argued that the 'cycle of deprivation' was a form of transmitted deprivation: not something new but now revealed because services had raised standards for most families, and 'revealed more clearly situations where standards had failed to rise' (Joseph, 1972a: 389). He argued that particular families produce subsequent generations of maladjusted people, and proposed:

1. The extension of family planning to reduce the numbers likely to be recruited into the 'cycle of deprivation';
2. Preparation for parenthood, to educate both children and adults;
3. Casework with emotionally deprived adults;
4. Playgroups to stimulate the development of the young; and
5. An overall strengthening of family life.

That this view reflected a prevailing one can be seen in the report published by the NSPCC in 1973 on its therapeutic playgroups (Rose, 1973). This was introduced by Arthur Morton, NSPCC Director, as follows:

> The establishment of over 50 playgroups during this period flows from the recognition of the extreme importance of the early years of life to the subsequent development and behaviour of human beings, the recognition of the 'cycle of deprivation' which passes inadequacy and suffering from one generation to the next. A cycle of inadequate parenthood, poverty, disablement and disturbance, clearly needs to be energetically attacked from a number of directions.

Sir Keith Joseph's proposals rely a good deal on the work of Mia Kellmer Pringle, then Director of the National Children's Bureau. In his speech to the NCB conference in 1972, Sir Keith remembered that he had increased their grant in the previous year as he greatly respected their work, and said:

> our links with the Bureau take the equally important form of close and friendly understanding between myself and my officers [at the DHSS] and your staff. I have had fruitful discussions with Dr Kellmer Pringle, and I think she knows that the Bureau has good friends within the Department . . . . I have given much thought to what Dr Kellmer Pringle and others have said to me. And I am fully aware that the ideas and new thinking that I want to promote derive much from what informed people in the child-care field have been urging for some time. (Joseph, 1972b: 4)

From 1972 onwards Sir Keith Joseph and Margaret Thatcher, then Minister of Education, carried out a series of consultations into parenting and the scope for helping people in the parental role, culminating in a seminar – 'The Family in Society: Dimensions of Parenthood' – in 1973, chaired by Joan Cooper as Director of the Social Work Service at the DHSS. Rutter (1974) cautioned the seminar on the extent to which intergenerational 'cycles of deprivation' could be said to occur, given the lack of evidence; nevertheless, their reality was the main assumption of the seminar. Cooper in her introduction, and Bronfenbrenner in his paper, put forward a picture of the family, and therefore society, as in crisis: child abuse and neglect were associated with families weakened by working mothers, absent fathers, declining extended families and decaying neighbourhoods (Bronfenbrenner, 1974).

This DHSS seminar drew together the establishment in the child welfare and social-work fields, including Kellmer Pringle, Joan Court (ex-NSPCC, then DHSS Social Work Service; see Chapter 3), Olive Stevenson, a social-work academic who would be a key member of the Maria Colwell Inquiry during the same year, and Priscilla Young of the Central Council for Education and Training in Social Work. In drawing together influential people, it simultaneously legitimated their views and gave influence and authority to the emerging Conservative agenda on the family and the welfare state.

The 'cycle of deprivation' became – despite a lack of empirical evidence and great ideological and political differences between members of the establishment – a way of handling the discourse around the family and social problems. It formed a theoretical underpinning to the gradual shift from universal to targeted services: targeting scarce resources on families at risk seemed sensible, and the (old) idea of using playgroups and social centres to involve and teach less competent parents was reaffirmed. The theory is vague enough to be acceptable across a wide spectrum, for it appears to link emotional, behavioural and environmental factors. The poverty lobby (e.g. Holman, 1978; Townsend, 1974, 1979) and the British Association of Social Workers challenged both the underlying ideology and the dubious empirical basis of the theory, but in practice the term became widely used by childcare organizations and professionals. Given that the theory amalgamates parenting factors (e.g. as derived from Kempe's work) and environmental and material factors, it has a strong affinity with social work (see Chapter 6 for a fuller critique).

The theory is, of course, part of a broader view of the causes of problems: Coffield *et al.* carried out some ethnographic research into 'problem' families and of routes in and out of deprivation, and found that local government officials thought in the same terms: it was their conventional wisdom to assume that certain problem families on certain stigmatized housing estates epitomized the theory. Indeed, many of these officials:

> appeared to operate with a strongly psychiatric or psychological model of deprivation, where the main problems were seen to be those of disturbed personality, low intelligence or poor heredity. (Coffield *et al.*, 1981: 4)

In the 1970s, then, welfare organizations responded to the debate on parenting and social problems: those in the statutory sector were faced with rising demand they were hard pressed to meet, and so targeting became attractive. In the voluntary sector, organizations threatened by the new and large social services departments began looking for new, community-based and politically validated areas of work. Both sectors conceived of playgroups and similar projects as the way to reach 'less than adequate' mothers.

Kellmer Pringle's work on *The Needs of Children* (1974), commissioned by Sir Keith Joseph, became a standard textbook for social workers and pre-school workers. Her brief had been to focus on the twin themes of the cycle of deprivation and preparation for parenthood in order to tackle transmitted deprivation. She argued that ignoring children's need for love and security had the consequences of filling prisons, mental hospitals and schools for the maladjusted, and swelling the numbers of the 'able misfits' (Kellmer Pringle, 1974: 81). A more daunting picture of motherhood should, she suggested, replace the idealized picture. She argued that the environment is of overriding importance and insisted that it is the experience of family life which needs to be improved through a programme of preparation for parenthood. Using work by Court (1969), Kempe (1962), Skinner and Castle (1969) on child abuse, and by Rutter (1974), West and Farrington (1971, 1973) on delinquency and maladjustment, she argued that parental inadequacy is likely to be repeated in the next generation.

Kellmer Pringle's key achievement was to assert the priority of parental duties and responsibilities over the 'politically fashionable' emphasis on parental rights amongst social workers (Kellmer Pringle, 1974: 105, 139). This shift was reflected in the 1975 Children Act, which made it easier to release children for adoption and was intended to improve planning in the lives of children in Care. The National Children's Bureau went on, with DHSS funding, to draw up a review and subsequently to develop initiatives into parent education in schools, adult education classes, antenatal classes, playgroups and parent support groups (Pugh, 1980). It also led to the Parker report (1980) on children separated from their families (discussed in the last chapter), which redefined the purpose of daycare as strategic – teaching better parenting – rather than just as a direct benefit for child or parent.

Breaking the 'cycle'

In the early 1970s the voluntary childcare organizations needed to find a new role for themselves, given the creation and subsequent expansion of statutory social services departments. There is a resonance between many of the ideas of the voluntary movement and those of Conservatism: mistrust of professions and large state-run organizations, a value on the family and its privacy, self-help, service and mutual aid (the neo-traditional view). Yet there is also a strong link with the Low Church strand of Labour, especially when these ideas are linked to the principles of social justice, citizenship and equity. In both strands questions of gender, and of the line between voluntary organizations and volunteer (i.e. free, non-professional) services, are fudged. We must also be mindful of the fact that the voluntary organizations have diverse roots in different doctrines, so that some have been more eager than others to pick up the discourse on the 'cycle of deprivation' on the Conservatives' familist terms; others have placed more stress on social and environmental factors, and been critical of low levels of social provision.

Richard Whitfield is an example of the neo-traditionalist view; as Director of Child Care at Save the Children Fund, he was prominent in the *Preparation for Parenthood Group* with Kellmer Pringle in the 1970s and with the *Exploring Parenthood* project with Hugh Jolly, a paediatrician. At a conference organized by the National Children's Home in 1978 on 'Education for Family Life: Towards Preventive Policies for Child Care', he gave a paper on 'Educating for Family Responsibility' in which he said:

> On our doorsteps, or more correctly, by our firesides, there is a growing crisis in the here and now which affects the quality of life for us today as the elemental building blocks of our social order – ordinary families – come under increasing stress as a result of changing ethics, economics, and health, education and welfare provision . . . children are harmed daily because the parents either stumbled almost unconsciously into parenthood, or because, in response to complex social pressures, they feel they have no alternative but to express resentment towards their children. Apparently overcome by responsibilities which they had not anticipated, and do not know how to tackle, often feeling isolated from opportunities for their own further development and personal fulfillment, they vent their frustration directly or indirectly on their offspring. Some repeat, through an apparent lack of alternative models, the harsh treatment which they suffered two decades previously from their own parents. (Whitfield, 1979)

At the same conference Patrick Jenkin, then Conservative spokesman on the Social Services, argued that the family was being undermined by working mothers, divorce, television, geographical mobility and rising expectations, with consequent delinquency, vandalism, child abuse and loss of parental authority. He said that 'ben-evolent and well-meaning intervention' in the family would only undermine it: indirect approaches which would strengthen family life and parental responsibility were necessary, such as tax arrangements to discourage mothers from working, involvement of parents in schools, leaving children with parents however adverse the circumstances, and other measures to encourage families to stand up to bureaucracy and officialdom (Barritt, 1979).

Parental involvement in primary schools

During the Labour administration of 1974–9, educational disadvantage was a strong theme. At the DES conference on the subject held in 1975 were Bridget Plowden, author of the influential report on *Children and Their Primary Schools* (1967) (which had led to the establishment of educational priority areas and compensatory educational programmes in areas of social disadvantage), Sir Alec Clegg and Jack Tizard, all prominent social democratic educationalists. Consistent with Labour Party views, they advocated a greater role for professionals in the education of both children and their parents, as well as greater cooperation between education and social services (DES, 1975: 7). A similar combination of adult education and educational home visiting was advocated in the Russell Report (1973), which encouraged schools to liaise with adult education institutes. Many local authorities went on to develop this kind of informal adult education, usually aimed at mothers, introducing them to new methods of schoolteaching, but also – as in the case of the Inner London Education Authority Family Workshops – providing crèches for children and seeking to open opportunities to women in their own right as well as involving them in their children's educational progress. For others, however, there was a strong welfare element to these classes, with mothers referred by health visitors, focus on parenting difficulties, and teaching by, for instance, Marriage Guidance or Samaritans counsellors as well as adult educators. This range offers an important parallel to family centres: from the supervised involvement of users in the social work/child protection model to the potential of opportunity and autonomy in the neighbourhood, community development and service models.

The 'post-Plowden orthodoxy' during the mid 1970s was that parental participation in primary schooling was a 'good thing'. Parental involvement was seen as the key variable in the relationship between social class and attainment, and to encourage such involvement many authorities have since established pre-school educational home visiting schemes. Some are based in adult education institutes, some in nursery schools or voluntary organizations; others are run jointly with social services departments or community health services. Some concentrate on families with severe problems, others visit all families in a given catchment area; some use volunteers, others use professionals such as adult education tutors. All aim to stimulate the parents' interest in and understanding of their child and his or her development, to relieve the stress and isolation of mothers, and to enable them to deal more effectively with school and professionals. While the Plowden Report is remembered for its stress on environmental deprivation and its recommendation of educational priority areas, its conclusion was that parental attitude is the most important dimension of children's progress (Halsey, 1972). One way of affecting this is to loosen the boundaries between home and school, to encourage parents to come into the school and the children to take books home – to interrelate adult and children's education, an idea central to the genesis of family centres.

The Red House Education Centre in Yorkshire, part of the National Education Priority Project, was opened in 1970 with services to the whole area to avoid stigmatizing parents who used it. The home visitor called weekly at the children's homes to discuss their development with the mothers, aiming to extend their 'natural' teaching role and understanding of schooling. Mothers liked the home visiting scheme, and involvement in Red House was high. Mothers of disadvantaged children were found to be interested in and capable of active involvement in the Red House group activities, and the informal and uncritical home visiting encouraged them. However, the boundaries between the home visitor and the social worker can blur, and Poulton and James (1975) commented that there were some mothers who had multiple problems or were too emotionally disturbed to look at their child's educational needs.

The pre-school playgroup movement

Involving mothers of pre-school children had become the 'obvious' response to poor parenting, educational failure and delinquency during the 1970s. At the 'Low Cost Day Provision for the Under-Fives' conference in 1976 organized by the DES and DIISS (which brought together Labour Party policy-makers and the child-care establishment) Rae Price, then Director of Islington's social services department, said:

> a striking example of our own local experience has been the capacity of individuals and groups classified as 'deprived', 'socially incompetent' who have increasingly taken over the management of their own playgroups whether it be in homeless family tenement blocks or in alienated problem estates. The participation of the mothers in pre-school activity has soon generalised out into a wider interest in their neighbourhood affairs . . . .The role of pre-school provision as a point of intervention into the cycle of deprivation is an extremely important one . . . .(DHSS/DES 1976: 38)

Emerging as a middle-class alternative to scarce nursery classes in 1961, the Pre-School Playgroups Association has attracted funding and recognition at both national and local level. Its playgroups are run with parental involvement and a minimum of paid workers; they are successful self-help organizations, catering for about half a million pre-school children, as many as attend all other forms of pre-school provision (Finch, 1984). Chairmen [sic] of the PPA have included Bridget Plowden and Mia Kellmer Pringle, placing it at the centre of the childcare and education establishment. The significance of the movement is not so much in the service it provides to children as in its self-proclaimed function in strengthening family and community life. With this aim, as well as that of providing a form of low-cost, self-help pre-school service, the DHSS has promoted playgroups. A senior DHSS officer wrote in 1973:

> The PPA . . . maintains that the children are helped mainly through their mothers. Playgroups can help in this way to strengthen and improve the influence of the family; only when the family is strengthened can there be lasting and important changes for the child. This strengthening of the family is particularly important in working with families with multiple problems. The play-group movement is often described as a middle class movement, but that this is no longer an accurate description is borne out by the PPA's success in involving problem family mothers in deprived areas. (Thayer, 1973)

The DHSS/DES conference on 'Low Cost Day Provision' focused on childminding, playgroups and voluntary organizations

and although it represented the Fabian/social democratic thinking of the time it nevertheless showed a certain affinity with
Conservative concerns with self-help and volunteering. Plowden,
as Chairman of the PPA, contrasted the growth of the voluntary
organizations with the inadequate provision of the statutory
sector, arguing that the vast expansion in nursery education
recommended in her Report (1967) would be better provided by
the voluntary sector. Furthermore, she argued:

> There is one resource which has *not* been used, but which
> the growth of professionalism has slowly been undermining,
> the mothers – and fathers – of small children and the
> community to which they belong, the confidence of parents
> in themselves . . . has been lessened . . . .We have to affirm
> the value of families (of one or two parents) and in particular
> of the mother–child relationship and the need to uphold,
> support and build on this relationship. (DHSS/DES, 1976:
> 17).

She argued that poor parenting caused crime:

> RecentlyIwastoldbyaseniormemberofthePrisonServicethatthe
> bestwaytoemptytheprisonswouldbetoseethatmothersweretaught
> how to handle their children. (*ibid.*: 41)

At the same conference Kellmer Pringle argued that playgroups
should be seen as preventive services in the field of mental
health, and that:

> positive discrimination can be given to vulnerable families
> and to children who are 'at risk', whether because of home
> circumstances or because of a mental or physical disability . . .
> Wherever possible, help should be given through and with
> the close involvement of the parent, especially the mother.
> (DHSS/DES, 1976: 54)

Playgroups, then, are about maternal education and involvement. Informal and voluntary 'resources', they supposedly
prevent mental illness, crime and child abuse because they
strengthen the family. PPA publications make this very clear:

> Anything that improves the mother's health and happiness
> has a profound effect upon her husband and children. The
> child grows twice over: he grows physically, emotionally,
> socially and intellectually through his playgroup experience

and comes home to continue growing in a happier, fuller home life than before. This wave of improvement flows yet again, for as the parents see their child developing in so many ways, their pleasure and interest grow both in him and in their shared experience as parents, and they both feel they are making out creditably. (Crowe, 1983: 3)

The PPA claimed that its playgroups were just as applicable to poor as to middle-class areas, and the DHSS encouraged the Association to extend its playgroups to work with deprived families. Research has raised doubts about these claims, showing that the most deprived people tend to make little use of playgroups, and in any case would prefer to see professionals rather than people like themselves providing what they feel their children need (Ferri and Niblett, 1977; Finch, 1984; Joseph and Parfit, 1972).

Home-Start

Other schemes – of which family centres were to be an example – have concentrated on these very demoralized mothers, and most have been influenced by Margaret Harrison's work in establishing Home-Start in Leicester in 1973. Home-Start, like Home Link in Liverpool and SCOPE in Southampton, uses volunteers who visit the homes of families under stress, to support the mothers and improve life for the children. All the volunteers are mothers themselves, and from varied backgrounds, the idea being that a 'mum-to-mum' approach is established. They attend a ten-week part-time course in child development and the social-work approach, and go on to visit families with very severe environmental and material problems, many of whom have neglected or abused their children.

The project was influenced by Bronfenbrenner's finding that only those compensatory education projects in the American Head-Start programme which involved mothers simultaneously with their children showed a lasting effect (Harrison, 1981). The application for Urban Aid for Home-Start was submitted when the DHSS was considering the 'cycle of deprivation' amid an assumption that the family was 'in crisis'. At the 1973 DHSS seminar Bronfenbrenner had advocated 'parent–child support systems' in poor neighbourhoods (Bronfenbrenner, 1974). Home-Start fitted the model. The DHSS Social Work Service Officer concerned wrote in a magazine circulated amongst the newly established social services departments:

> In 1972–3 as a result of wide consultation about the problem of the 'cycle of deprivation', a great deal of support was found for the view that many of the children under five and their parents who were most in need could best be reached by taking services into their own homes. (Corsellis, 1977: 10)

Since the DHSS and DES did not wish to increase the workload of health visitors, social workers or teachers, the volunteer element was attractive to them, and when the Leicester Council for Voluntary Service submitted the application for Urban Aid for their Home-Start project, the DHSS was 'greatly interested' (*ibid.*: 10).

The aim of the project was to 'break the cycle of deprivation by encouraging the less adequate mothers to help their pre-school childen', and:

> to build on the parent as the sustaining agent and on the home as the sustaining background . . . to focus on the parent rather than the child, thus the parent is encouraged to realize her worth as expert for her child . . . to encourage physical and verbal contact between mother and child . . . to encourage self-respect . . . to encourage language development, sensory stimulation, play, independence and outings locally . . . to encourage the use of community resources. (*ibid*: 11)

Home-Start was evaluated by Van der Eyken (1982) for the DHSS and SSRC, and the evaluation is published by the offshoot of Home-Start, the Home-Start Consultancy, which received government funding to disseminate the Home-Start approach. It was also discussed in National Children's Bureau work, notably by Pugh (1980) on parent education. In his foreword to Van der Eyken's book, Sir Patrick Nairne, former Permanent Secretary at the DHSS, said that Home-Start had particularly impressed him because:

> Firstly it is based upon an idea of remarkable and attractive simplicity: a bond of friendship between one mother and

another, usually between a mother who has learned to cope and a younger mother who is finding it hard to do so. Secondly, it is a notably inexpensive scheme – with the volunteer mother unpaid and requiring only modest training. (Van der Eyken, 1982: xv)

Van der Eyken describes Home-Start families in terms of the classic problem family:

generally highly alienated people; often lonely, depressed and deeply suspicious, even fearful of both services and service givers, whom they perceived as threatening their own weak sense of identity. We particularly observed their own lack of a 'sense of control'; they felt that they were not masters [sic] of their fate but, conversely, that they were victims of a manipulative world in which their own actions had almost no consequence. Moreover, these families were often isolated socially, with the mothers sometimes displaying not only a lack of maternal and parenting skills, but also having difficulty in establishing more general relationships. (*ibid.*: vi)

Of the 303 families visited by Leicester Home-Start Volunteers during 1974–8, 90 per cent were on a very low income, 40 per cent were single parents, 25 per cent had children on the At Risk Register, 13 per cent were from ethnic minorities. Many were also in poor or overcrowded housing, were victims of physical or emotional battering (both mothers and children), were lonely or isolated, lacked any routine, suffered from poor health, were of low intelligence, were rejected by their close relatives, had children who lacked stimulating and new experiences and parents who had experienced deprived, unhappy childhoods or were emotionally bereft. Many of these families had rudimentary or non-existent social networks: the volunteer is intended to be the first link in forming one.

The volunteers could come from any background as long as they were mothers themselves and attended a short course on child development and social work. Margaret Harrison writes of the spirit of altruism in motivating them, but she also sees them as people who need to be needed. This is what Van der Eyken (after Abrams, e.g. 1980) refers to as the reciprocity model of community care. While the volunteers give time to 'their' families, they receive back a recognition of their status as mother; after Winnicott (e.g. 1964), he talks of therapy as good mothering. So for the volunteers a bond is created and their own status is enhanced:

> Because they are not paid, the volunteers wield a con-siderable, though unspoken, moral authority within the families they support, tacitly recognized by those families by the fact that few, if any, relationships break down. (Van der Eyken, 1982: 63)

The moral authority of mother, teacher and therapist, then, powerfully combine. The visitors teach mothers to cook, to budget, to sew and to care better for their children. They arrive with play materials and provide a role model of good mothering. The length of service is notable: 46 per cent of volunteers were still involved with the project at the end of the four years studied by Van der Eyken. Their social background was diverse, though the busier volunteers were more likely to be active church members, and these volunteers, unlike non-church members, were also likely to be involved in other projects. The church group was less likely to be in paid employment than the non-church group, having both more time and a strong sense of commitment.

Conclusion: parents as partners

In her research on education and motherhood, David (1985) noted the overlap of education and welfare surveillance, under-lining the way in which adult education and home visiting are predicated on the assumption that the normal mother is inter-ested in her child's education and wants him/her to succeed. Those who do not conform to this assumption become the target of a social-work approach which tries to change their behaviour. I have shown that under the Conservatives, and especially Sir Keith Joseph, there was a strong focus on apparently deviant or disaffected families: they (and they only) should be the target of state services. The Labour Party in the 1970s was also becoming more selective in its social policies, but it did not share the Conservatives' dislike of professionals: they were not the problem but could be part of the solution if they worked more with voluntary and volunteer projects. Both parties were concerned with the family and with mothers: in tackling social problems, especially of educational failure, delinquency and mental illness, they sought to 'break the cycle' at the point of socialization – by changing mothers' behaviour.

A certain area of common ground must be established for policy to be created: around it there is a shifting and more contentious area. So in all the official discourse (Burton and Carlen, 1979) on educational disadvantage, the 'cycle of deprivation' and child abuse in the 1970s one finds little reference to the sexual politics or issues of violence to women being raised at the time by the women's movement. I have argued that social policy is not an outcome of a single political party or dominant ideology, but is created from a shifting consensus formed and re-formed by an establishment drawn from an elite of the professions and political parties. The establishment in the childcare field which we have discussed is drawn from diverse backgrounds of Left and Right, yet its common focus was that the family (not gender relations or resource issues or the quality and extent of daycare and family services) was the appropriate target and focus of discussion and action. The language of class is replaced by the notion of disadvantage – obscuring the real differences in social position between parents, and fudging issues to do with the politics of state welfare and poverty.

The 1970s, then, saw a stress on parental involvement in state services, some of which came from parents themselves (as with the care of children with special needs, discussed in Chapter 3), and some from professionals and voluntary organizations who were facing changed circumstances, given the new and large social services departments. Political parties were keen to focus on the family in order to break the cycle of educational disadvantage, delinquency and offending, and child abuse; and local authorities needed to look to voluntary agencies, volunteers, and the resources of families and communities to meet rising demand for social care services for children as well as elderly, mentally ill and disabled people – a demand which was rising with the closure of large insitutions. Participation of parents, partnership with parents, shared care, became key words.

What parental involvement policies mean in practice is problematic: the deviant mother's involvement in a project is supervised, her partnership brings her under surveillance. The efficient mother acts as a responsible auxiliary to the professional, becomes a volunteer worker herself, and perhaps finds a new autonomy and set of opportunities in her life. However, we see in targeted and selective programmes like Home-Start, and some educational home visiting schemes, a supervision of mothers, a denial of the autonomy that use of services on demand might promote. The especial moral authority of the volunteer distinguishes these projects from those where participation is as an equal, a peer, or as a citizen – for instance in schools, or in respite care for disabled children (or the service model of family centres). These issues of the manner of mothers' involvement in projects are central to family centres, as we showed in Chapter 2, and will pervade the remaining chapters of this book. The context of involvement is important: rather than coercive state intervention into families, at present we see a neglect of families, and especially of women and children. Mothers whose major problems are poverty and housing may *have* to participate in schemes such as Home-Start for lack of alternative services, and some may struggle to run playgroups with pitiful resources – the exploitative participation we see in some neighbourhood family centres.

Much social work with families is essentially about taking middle-class ideas of pedagogy (and, we might add, of physical and emotional well-being) to working-class families. What liberates the middle-class family might not 'work' in different social conditions and once it is attached to state surveillance of poor families. This question of social welfare's potential to liberate or merely to regulate is one we shall return to in Chapters 6 and 7. Now we turn to social workers themselves, asking how they negotiated the waters of the discourse on the 'cycle of deprivation' and the challenge to break it: the discourse from which family centres have emerged.

CHAPTER 5

SOCIAL WORK AND FAMILY CENTRES

In this chapter I shall consider the influence of social work on the development, shape and functioning of family centres. I shall look at various strands of social work, especially family therapy and community work, and assess their influence on the development of family centres. Social work will be seen as having relative autonomy in the marketplace of ideas, and as a profession characterized by several segments of varying influence and ideology. I have already noted that social work's task is changing, moving beyond the traditional character work with 'problem families' to the development and 'support' of informal caring in family and community. Social work is currently caught in a pincer movement: the low level of public daycare and community care services makes the task of supporting families harder; at the same time, public interest in child abuse raises the stakes for social work, especially as the material factors which may exacerbate child abuse – poverty, poor housing – are themselves growing. In this context, how has social work influenced the development of family centres, the translation of policy into practice, and what are the implications for their – mainly women – users?

Professional dominance?

In family centres the principle of participation is stressed, yet there are differences in the understanding of what participation might mean – differences which cannot be explained by bureaucratic qualities such as whether the centre is in the statutory or voluntary sector, for centres vary as much within these categories as between them. The rough guide of neighbourhood or social work/child protection centres does not explain why, amongst the local authority social services centres studied, there was variety in attitude to parental involvement. The voluntary-sector centres studied ranged from closed therapeutic centres to centres stressing the social benefit of daycare and seeking to be accessible to a wide range of groups in the community, although none went so far as some of the Children's Society and Save the Children Fund centres which sought to empower local residents (see, for instance, Holman's [1983] account of Children's Society family centres).

Some of the reasons for the decline and discrediting of the service approach have been considered in earlier chapters: rationing and restricted expenditure, political encouragement of voluntary organizations to work to break the 'cycle of deprivation' and 'welfare dependence' in families by forms of parent education and treatment. Social work as a profession has also had a role in shaping this area of work, and of pulling away from a straightforward service approach based on children rather than parents. While social work is a relatively weak profession (compared to law or medicine), in family centres we see instances of social workers controlling (at the local level) the terms, conditions and content (Freidson, 1970) of their work. While social work cannot be said to have the autonomy of an ideal-type profession, it does exercise considerable delegated discretion – which poses problems for its management and raises classic professional–bureaucracy tensions. Researching social workers in the childcare field of social services departments, Packman observed:

> Despite the formal hierarchies, the bureaucratic organization charts and the social workers' own perception that they crouched at the bottom of a very heavy heap, cramped and restricted by rules and regulations, the picture, as we understood it, was very different. What we saw were social workers with considerable potential autonomy, at least in so far as decisions about child admissions [to Care] were concerned, and the power that comes in part from being the prime holders of vital information . . . and also from working at the boundary between the organization and the outside

world. In this, social workers seemed to us to belong to the
species 'street-level bureaucrat' identified by American
sociologists and to be found not only in social-welfare
organizations, but also in the police-force, in teaching . . . .
(Packman *et al*, 1986: 11–12)

Satyamurti (1981) also noted the considerable delegated discretion and scope for interpreting policy which social workers actually wield in their practice. Professions can be understood as interest groups which, as they seek to expand their domain, need allies. They seek a control of relevant discourses, the right to speak with authority on certain social problems, and a mandate to work within that field or domain. The state is a crucial party – as we showed in the last chapter – in the sponsoring of professions, in the creation and legitimation of an establishment within them and across certain fields such as childcare (Johnson, 1972).

Professional dominance, however, has strict limits. The manoeuvring of professions such as social work may be mainly local, unless it is allied to more powerful professions such as law or medicine. While left libertarians in the early 1980s painted a picture of an expanding social-work profession placing families 'increasingly "at risk" of state intervention' (Geach and Szwed, 1983: 1), reality, especially by the late 1980s, was somewhat different. There are resource as well as cultural factors inhibiting expansion. The social workers in my research tended to refer to labelling theory: keeping people out of the welfare system was a powerful part of their larger aim to prevent the development of deviant careers. Social workers, as Packman (1986) found, operate the 'rule of pessimism': they view their own services as stigmatizing – being in Care or attending a day nursery are to be avoided where possible for the client's sake. Dingwall *et al.* (1983) offer the 'rule of optimism' as another barrier to intrusive social work: social workers (like the rest of us) operate within a frame that says parents normally love their children: something very exceptional must occur to shift them to a view that parents are so pathological that statutory intervention is necessary.

However, professions are not homogeneous and there are internal debates on principles and values. I have already noted the generally pessimistic attitudes to day and residential care amongst social workers, but such an attitude is not universally held. For instance, in surveying preventive policies amongst social services departments in 1985 for the British Association of Social Workers (BASW), Tunstill found considerable variation as to goals and a lack of clarity as to what the term meant and how it might be made operational. She therefore argued, on behalf of BASW, that prevention should mean:

> (i) making available resources and advice to prevent children being separated from their families by enforced reception into care; (ii) redefining local authority care as a positive resource to be used by some families when a break is needed, not a sanction imposed on them by society in the shape of social workers; (iii) the early and sensitive rehabilitation of children in their own families; and (iv) the maintenance of links between members of a family where parents care about their children, but are not able on a daily basis to care for them.
>
> The last three of these entail the need for social workers to stop seeing reception into care as a sign of failure on the part of parents. (Tunstill, 1985: 15)

There is not 'a' social work view, then, but different subcultures and a moving context within which debate takes place.

Family therapy, social work and family centres

The early 1970s, despite the innovative social services departments and a concomitant expansion in training and status for social workers, was a time of cutbacks in public expenditure, and critiques of state welfare from both Right and Left. A mood of uncertainty, especially amongst managers of social services departments, was underscored by the media interest in the child abuse inquiries. Leadership by the NSPCC and paediatricians on the issue of child abuse, and an interest in the new techniques of family therapy amongst social workers, shaped the dominant discourse on child protection from the mid 1970s (see Chapter 3). While the poverty lobby and the community-work segment of social work also put forward views on child abuse – emphasizing situational factors and deprivation – their discourse was overshadowed by the more powerful (because of its elite connections) medical and psychopathological model. Being silent on issues of class, culture or gender, this model has had affinities with (though it is far from identical with) the New Right's new stress on parental responsibility.

Family therapy became an 'obvious' way for social services departments and family centres to be seen to be doing something about child abuse. It had neither the more nebulous goals of community work, nor some of its political conflicts. It could provide a means of working with families and children identified as 'at risk', and of being sanctioned by the medical profession. Thus it was that services for children became (or reverted to?) services aimed at parents, an approach stated clearly by Kempe, the leading 'discoverer' of the battered baby whose ideas were introduced to the UK by the NSPCC (see Chapter 3):

> Long-term treatment may involve a relationship with a social worker who gives support of a practical and emotional kind, with a lay therapist who enables the parent to trust and feel valued as an individual, or with an analyst or psychotherapist who explores the patient's past in once or twice-weekly sessions. This course is more complicated and often more difficult for the parent to accept than the emergency treatment. And yet it is clearly here that any real hope of reducing the incidence of child abuse must lie. (Kempe and Kempe, 1978: 91–2)

From 1973 onwards, paediatricians and psychiatrists pushed psychotherapy for parents as the solution to the problem of child abuse. This approach also meshed with the critique of Care: children would no longer be rescued from bad parents, and further damaged in Care, but families as a whole would be treated and monitored. It could be – as Pfohl (1977) suggests – that, given that professions draw status from their clientele, for childcare professionals to move from working with children to adults might mean greater status and intellectual interest.

It is ironic that working to keep families together seemed so 'new'. The NSPCC had promoted family reform at the end of the last century, and social workers had been working with families to keep children out of Care since the 1948 Children Act by supporting parents. In 1960 the Ingleby Report on *Children and Young Persons* reaffirmed these practices and noted that the local authority children's departments were indeed working in a spirit of prevention, assisting poor families. The 1963 Children and

Young Persons Act made it a duty of local authorities to promote the welfare of children (in order to prevent delinquency and entry to Care) by helping families as a whole. The Ingleby Report had suggested the establishment of family advice centres, and a few children's departments did establish them in areas of high social need. As Holman (1988: 45) says, 'they did not become widespread but they served as forerunners of a means of prevention to become popular two decades later'.

Those social workers who began working in the child protection field from the mid 1970s onwards, then, did so in a milieu where the practice of vague support for families was becoming increasingly questioned, in terms of its effectiveness, its politics, and its cost. Mobilization around the issue of child abuse brought a degree of patronage from the more powerful paediatricians and psychiatrists; at the same time, the more cosmopolitan of social workers (Blau and Scott, 1963) looked to the therapies which were being developed in the United States. The family therapy movement has blossomed since that time: it includes clinical psychologists, psychotherapists and social workers. The Association for Family Therapy was established in Britain in 1976, with regular conferences, a journal, and a burgeoning theoretical and clinical literature. Few social workers practise purely as family therapists; rather, they work in settings such as family centres or child guidance clinics which enable them to use this method.

> Like many social workers, when I encountered family therapy, I embraced it eagerly and lovingly – and pretty uncritically. Here were methods, explicit and direct techniques for change, ways to work, ways to think. It had a conceptual framework – systems theory – a structure from which to view behaviour and to tackle symptoms. And it did not take for ever to see change occur. For the first time I felt truly instrumental in my professional functioning. Now I was not 'merely' a social worker – I was a family therapist. It had a more authoritative ring to it. (Walters, 1990: 15)

Family therapy offers training, an international academic literature, research and evaluation, and prestigious conferences and seminars – prestigious in that the 'big names' from medicine are involved (Zawada, 1981). It dissociates social work from its open-ended, supportive casework tradition, and gives the social worker a goal-orientated method. It is widespread in family centres, and has continued to be the preeminent approach – at the expense of community work and the service model. Much of the terminology used in discussing families is recognizable to insiders as family therapeutic categories and concepts: 'parent/child system', 'effective interaction', 'coping ability', 'serious malfunction', 'problem-solving'. Part 'psychobabble', part systems theory, part behaviourism, this is the control-talk that Cohen (1985) calls 'technobabble', the argot of the helping, healing and punishing professions.

Family therapy has developed fast. Grove Place Family Centre (a former children's home) worked like this:

> A basic rule is that parents are always responsible for their children while they are with them in the Centre. [Staff] . . . act as resources for the parents, encouraging, challenging, supporting and confronting them in their care of their children. An overall aim is to create an environment in which it is possible for families to change and acquire and practice new skills. (Centre document)

In Grove Place we find a classic example of the street-level discretion referred to above: the organizer was a social worker who, like his staff, had done further training in family therapy, and was well integrated in family therapy networks. He said that there was sufficient vagueness on the local authority committee and amongst the senior managers of his social services department for him to work in the way he thought right. As long as the committee knew they were getting a child protection service they would leave him to shape that service; only one councillor had raised the issue of the concomitant loss of general childcare services.

Family therapy has several roots: the social psychiatry of Maxwell Jones, which uses group processes to overcome institutionalization and to improve communication (Jones, 1968); the anti-psychiatry of Laing, which attempts to uncover distortions in family relations (Laing and Esterson, 1964); child psychoanalysis – which, from Freud onwards, has sought the seeds of the child's symptoms in the parent – as developed by Bowlby (e.g. 1952) and Winnicott (1964). The American influences have been the systems approach and Bateson's work on communication, and there is the influential Milan school (see Walrond-Skynner [1979] for a summary). The range of roots and philosophies within family therapy have led many practitioners to refer to it as an eclectic field (Zawada, 1981): the St Michael's organizer said that the methods he found useful were systems theory, family therapy, community work, group-work, behaviour modification, task-centred work and the use of contracts. Family therapy, then, is probably more easily seen as a set of social practices which broadly assume that child disturbance and child abuse have their roots in parental malfunctioning and pathology; it does not seek to understand such pathology in its own right but to see how pathological patterns of interaction in the family system have led to the victimization of a (child) member. As systems theory, it assumes that a change in one part of the system will have knock-on effects into other parts. In principle it works with the whole family; but in the overwhelming majority of centres I have researched it is the women of the family who attend: 'engaging' men is an acknowledged problem.

Family therapy, then, contains strange bedfellows: behaviourism combined with growth therapies and psychoanalysis. Walrond-Skynner argues that while all family therapy is based on general systems theory, there is a distinction between:

> those schools of family therapy which concentrate on assisting the family group to change by acquiring some insight into areas of its dysfunction (dynamic, Bowenian and experiential schools), and those schools of family therapy which concentrate on helping the family to change its patterns of behaviour without increasing its awareness of dysfunctional processes (strategic, communicational and behavioural). (Walrond-Skynner, 1979: 2)

For family therapists (or would-be family therapists) these philosophical and methodological differences do not undermine the unity of this field, and there has been considerable activity to promote family therapy more broadly. For instance, at the fifth Annual Conference for Family Therapy, Bill Jordan argued that the application of family therapy within social services departments had hitherto been too limited. Despite 'the very evident devotion and enthusiasm for the method amongst many social workers', relatively few families actually receive family therapy (Jordan, 1981; Treacher and Carpenter, 1984). Social worker family therapists, then, need settings such as family centres in which to practise.

The primary care, 'nurturing' approach of Kempe, introduced into the UK by the NSPCC in the early 1970s, has recently been heavily criticized. An example of this older approach is seen in the Market Family Centre, which is a

> refuge with regular meals, caring and attention to help families weather the immediate crisis and then to think about their more long-standing problems. Working as a team, we offer families the time to talk and reflect about themselves and their relationships in regular counselling sessions. We also offer children and adults the chance to learn to express their needs and develop new creative ways of meeting them in groups and informal settings. The primary care team responds to the day-to-day needs of parents and children as they come in and encourages their use of the time and our resources. Sometimes the most primary kinds of response are called for: feeding, cuddling, bathing, playing, just being with . . . people at their most deprived and needy. (Centre document)

By the mid 1980s such an approach was under threat, again with NSPCC leadership:

> Before the 1970's . . . [influenced by Henry Kempe] Workers tended to acknowledge the powerlessness of the parents to influence their own affairs and would accept the responsibility for producing change. Thus dependency was deliberately encouraged. . . . (Dale, 1984: 12)

Dale continued by noting empirical research which casts doubt on the effectiveness of such 'nurturant' therapy (Baher *et al.*, 1976), and argued that there was a danger of workers becoming enmeshed in the minutiae of these families' lives, and losing objectivity. His NSPCC team in Rochdale used Gestalt and Transactional Analysis in its family therapy, emphasizing all the while the need for the adults to take responsibility for their own actions. The Rochdale team were quite different from the 'nurturing' centres:

> The assessment and therapeutic model of the Rochdale unit emphasizes a structured use of control in a therapeutic setting with non-voluntary clients. Therapeutic work is offered by a team – a specific group of either two, three, or four workers. Sessions during the three-month assessment

period are office based, by appointment, and time limited. Contracts are used to clarify for the family what the expectations of the team will be. The statutory order (always a care order) provides the mandate for the assessment work. For the purpose of eventual therapeutic progress we feel that it is essential that the authority of the team be emphasized clearly and specifically at the beginning of the assessment. (Dale, 1984; 13, see also Dale *et al.*, 1986)

Control and firm boundaries are part of the treatment, and seen as necessary for immature parents (Sheppard, 1982). Dale's paper was given at the International Congress on Child Abuse and Neglect in 1984: his model for assessment and intervention is derived from Bentovim's work at the Great Ormond Street Hospital; cosmopolitan and prestigious medical links legitimate and assist the dissemination of ideas. This tougher approach meshed with the trend towards a more authoritarian stance in childcare work in social services departments (Frost and Stein, 1989), and with Conservative policies based on parental responsibility. Employers had to be seen to be protecting children effectively and with clear goals, distancing themselves from the anxious family support and casework approach so castigated by Blom Cooper in the Jasmine Beckford Inquiry (London Borough of Brent, 1985). Directors of social services departments (who were to gain more influence in the training of social workers from 1989) emphasized monitoring and treatment rather than prevention and community social work. So what *did* happen to community work?

Community work and ecological approaches

As we have seen in previous chapters, parental involvement grew out of schemes such as playgroups which aimed to strengthen families and prevent children coming into Care. The twin of involvement is participation, a principle of many family centres, which has one of its roots in community work. As we saw in Chapter 2, community work has strongly influenced family centres, especially those of the neighbourhood and community development models (Adamson and Warren, 1983; Hasler, 1984;

Holman, 1983; Phelan, 1983). These family centres and their
voluntary organizations have all stressed their commitment to
enabling people living in poor communities to participate in
projects, and to increasing the strengths of such communities by
enhancing the capacities of individuals to enter into reciprocal
exchanges – the basis of a social network. Solidarity and
reciprocity: the projects are given to the community to catalyse
and promote change from below, in contrast to the paternalist
model of provision where professionals decide what is needed.
Community-work projects aim to enable those who are at risk of
social exclusion because of their inability to participate to give as
well as to take. They argue that the stigma that attaches to state
welfare projects lies in their unreciprocated taking: as Gouldner
(1973) said, those who want or need 'something for nothing' are
viewed as flawed, as not fully adult citizens.

Participation, then, has a central place in community work, but
it is fraught with difficulties: it has the purpose of helping
disadvantaged groups gain a better share of resources (rationing
by clamour [Thomas, 1983: 66]), but it is also an educational
process which enables participants to become more skilled and
knowledgeable and thus more effective on their own behalf. It is
common to find participation in the neighbourhood as valued in
itself, especially where 'lifestyle radicalism' and church projects
predominate.

Whether the end is localized or seen in broader terms,
community work sees participation as a process of empowerment.
Groups who, through poverty, cannot participate in the political
process, are, argues Thomas, effectively disenfranchised and,
like Holman, he argues for action to redress this. Participation is
seen as teaching and reinforcing political competence – a point
made in the Russell Report (1973) on *Adult Education*, which
advocated a greater commitment to adult education amongst
socially disadvantaged people. Thomas argues that community
work is concerned with the exercise and control of power and
responsibility:

> The taking of responsibility for defining one's own needs
> and the learning of skills and confidence to meet group goals,
> is a process of empowerment, as is the building of social
> relationships within a community and between different ˉ
> groups . . . . Joining in the activities of a community group set

on achieving a particular task is potentially a process of empowerment . . . .(Thomas, 1983: 129)

Empowerment has been strongly asserted by the Children's Society, which based its family centres in part on the Melbourne Family Project (Liffman, 1978). Its principles were deprofessionalization and participation by the families, with a transfer of skills from professionals to the families. Hasler (1984), of the Children's Society, argued for the principles of participation, openness and development, through a model of learning developed from that of Freire (1970), which stresses the aim of increasing the capacities of oppressed individuals and groups to change and control their environment. Hasler argued that family centre projects – which his review describes – must strive to enable people 'to do for' themselves, and that providing opportunities for this to occur means opening up agencies to their publics.

The ecological approach links community to family intervention, and in some cases explicitly to family therapy. This model sees individuals and groups as drawing resources from and making exchanges with their environment. It is an approach which has enabled family centre social workers to stress environmental factors – the poverty, poor housing, ill health, and so forth – of their clientele, but nevertheless to focus on the parenting behaviour and psychology of their clients. This approach, developed early at St Michael's, has influenced many family projects. There is a stress on social network, and on the place of the family centre in forming one: the users are often isolated people without 'normal' social ties in the community. Holman (1983), for instance, sees social stresses and inequality as the fundamental causes of child abuse, neglect and family breakdown – via social exclusion and low self-esteem and confidence – so he argues that the family centre should be a 'resourceful friend'.

Like family therapy, the ecological paradigm is an American import. Its critical features include Bronfenbrenner's notion of reciprocity: an active notion of individuals who shape their environments. He had called for a range of public services to support families in their child-rearing tasks at the DHSS seminar on 'Dimensions of Parenthood' in 1972–3, basing his call on the notion that families need to be able to interact with social support networks for their proper functioning (Bronfenbrenner, 1974).

The central idea in the ecological paradigm is that personal competence and the environment are dynamically linked: if there is a concern about parents' competence, then intervention must consist of life and social skills teaching to produce improved levels of personal competence, *combined with* community group-work aimed at improving social supports for children and families. In a sense this is – and has always been – the essence of social work: the focus on person-in-environment. Social support may occur in 'natural' helping networks, such as family or friendships, or in formed networks (e.g. self-help groups), or more formally through professionals and their agencies.

We can see that this paradigm fits family centres of all types: the neighbourhood model seeks to offer or to promote informal networks and self-help groups, whereas the social-work/child protection and service models are at the more formal end of the spectrum. All, though, are in some way looking at the competence of parents *and* at the resources they need to support them (see Whittaker *et al.*, 1986; Whittaker and Garbarino, 1983). As a paradigm it draws on several fields: cultural anthropology, the sociology of networks, social psychology, community health and psychiatry, and social medicine, with its focus on the interaction between individual and environment in the production of illness or health. In this country Rutter's work on resilience and vulnerability factors in the genesis of poor parenting (Rutter *et al.*, 1983), and Brown and Harris's (1978) on vulnerability and protective factors in the genesis of depression in women, have strengthened the model and influenced family centres.

This model has also influenced social services departments. From their creation in 1971 they promoted a form of community social work: the social worker was to develop the resources in and of the community networks (ensuring that the state did not pay for too many services which women could be encouraged to provide informally). The Barclay Report further promoted this idea in 1982, as did many social services departments which decentralized in the 1970s and 1980s in an attempt to work more closely with the 'natural caring forces' in the community (Hadley *et al.*, 1984). Social services departments' family centres are directly in this framework: the family centre helps women as *producers* (as well as consumers) of social care.

Family centres' social work

Family centres aim to strengthen families by altering the ecological balance of their environments. They provide support and resources, promote peer support, teach skills in parenting and seek to alter the behaviour of individual families. The balance of these two endeavours varies between centres, according to staff interests and their managing agency. The majority of centres I have observed, visited, or whose documents I have read, have, however, tended towards the behaviour-change end of the spectrum: six out of the ten centres studied for this research used family therapy. Warren (1990) found that at least half of the centres surveyed in his national study carried out intensive work with families. While all the centres in my study described themselves as a resource, the extent to which development work was done to increase the resources for informal groups was limited, though more marked in some of the neighbourhood centres. Nevertheless, the ecological paradigm makes it possible to see all family centre work as a defined field of social intervention, with their workers using a common framework, though some emphasize the personal, some the social and community.

Family centres reflect the framework of social work, but they also reflect organizational and professional needs of the last two decades. Social services departments needed to keep the numbers of children in Care down to contain their costs. Social workers 'needed' to carry out their child protection mandate with some confidence. Fells and de Gruchy (1991) looked at social workers' perceptions of family centres, asking them how they saw the centres as helping the families they worked with, and what additional services the families needed. The families concerned were poor – two-thirds were on income support and half had housing problems – yet it was parenting problems which had brought them to the attention of the social workers. While the social workers indicated that family centres were a priority, only 4 out of the 22 asked described anything like Holman's neighbourhood model. Eleven wanted the client-focused (social-work/child protection) model; the rest wanted a mixture. They wanted help for the emotional and relationship problems in families, for the isolation and vulnerability they saw: supportive and practical help, combined with advice on childcare, for families on their caseloads. They wanted such help for cases they felt they could not close because of anxiety about the welfare of the children – cases they could not help, but could not ignore. Family centres were perceived as offering practical help combined with more intensive help than social workers could offer.

Gibbons (1990) found that social workers were worried by the crisis work and the extent of need in 'their' families: asked what resources they wanted, they envisaged a specialist resource centre for whole families to be assessed and treated, and within which there could be planned and focused work (Gibbons, 1990: 138–40). Yet the social workers also stressed peer-group support; they saw this as preferable to the imposition of 'alien standards of childcare', and thought that such support could lead to a rehabilitation of families, who would move on to be able to join 'normal' playgroups. They thought the centre should be available, with as diverse a range of helping methods as possible, and flexible and accessible – especially for peer groups, and for compensatory care for children whose parents could not meet their needs. Fells and de Gruchy concluded that although the majority of social workers described the client-focused model, on balance the neighbourhood model was nearer to what they actually wanted for families. Gibbons noted that the decline in commitment to decentralized 'patch' community social work had left social workers feeling that community development work was a luxury and could be carried out only at the expense of 'their' families. This attitude is one born of the pressures on statutory social services departments as services to and benefits for poor families have contracted.

The client-focused, social-work family centre which social workers have tended to promote reflects in part, then, their organizational needs – somewhere to contain, monitor and treat what appear to be increasing numbers of 'dangerous' families, or families suffering multiple deprivation. It reflects their close knowlege of the conditions of life in families in poverty – hence the citing of the neighbourhood model when the need is looked at from the families' point of view. It also reflects professional interests: family therapy is intellectually stimulating and prestigious compared to the more mundane business of supporting families in practical and educative ways. So family therapy has become a strong model of practice in family centres: it meshes with the organizational need to treat and monitor families, and it is interesting to social workers. The neighbourhood model (which appears to be of more interest to the users) gets overshadowed, and the service approach is dismissed as essentially practical and of use only to monitor children, not to treat parents. For these reasons I shall go on to look at some critiques of family therapy, and specifically to consider the implication for women of its use in family centres. The neighbourhood and service models will be further considered in the next chapter.

Family centres, therapies and women users

During the 1950s and 1960s many noted the expansion of what Donzelot (1980) calls the 'psy' professons, and what Berger (1965) called the 'counselling and testing complex' around institutional psychiatry. Berger saw this as a reflection of a general (American) cultural acceptance of psychoanalytic ideas: they became part of the taken-for-granted in American society. Szasz (1970) argued that it has benefited psychiatrists to reclassify non-illness as illness, but while he places the responsibility for this reclassification of behaviour with psychiatry, he places the *demand* for psychotherapy in the 'deterioration' of privacy in the relationship between doctor and patient. The search for the private and personal physician took the form of the search for the analyst, the psychotherapist and – in the 1980s and 1990s – for alternative therapies as well as a range of counselling and psychotherapies.

While some, such as Halmos (1967), saw the 'rise of the counsellors' as a positive force, generalizing humane values of kindness, tolerance and permissiveness, others, such as Comfort (1967), were more sceptical about the 'anxiety makers'. Lasch (1979) has written of the culture of narcissism: a new self-absorption where, rather than sinking his identity in the future or in others, the modern narcissist expects immediate gratification of his impulses: to live for himself. Lasch sees this narcissism as a retreat from the political movements of the 1960s, a retreat into pseudo-authenticity and awareness.

While Europe may see fewer of these therapies than North America, there has clearly been a similar trend, and the interest amongst social workers in therapies and personal growth is marked. Raymond (1986), writing of the women's movement, says that we may talk of 'therapism', a phenomenon which means that a premium is placed on self-disclosure, which becomes a ritual, a way of life, with those who refuse to disclose being seen as repressed. This compulsion to disclose is in the tradition of the confession: Foucault (1976) points out that confession is an obligation not only in religion but in justice, medicine and education, and also in love and family relationships. Self-help groups also embody this confession; Robinson's (1979) research into Alcoholics Anonymous shows how the new entrant to the group must go through a process akin to a religious conversion: despair, seeing the light, hope, confession, penance, respon-sibility. Confession and conversion have their modern forms in psychotherapy: the client/patient comes to share the profes-sional's view of the problem (if it is 'successful'). Wootton (1977) has shown how, in group therapy, the term 'sharing' is used to describe meaningful discussion, yet professionals adjudicate as to what is or is not meaningful, exerting their power through their interpretations, with the patient learning what to talk about and in what manner. This culture – and the emphasis on personal growth and self-disclosure – was evident in seven out of the ten family centres I studied, with older staff from former regimes being edged out or moving on if they did not fit.

What was noticeable in my research was also the commitment to feminist values – loosely speaking – among the women social workers interviewed, yet within their practice we see something at odds with feminism. Women users are targeted; childcare problems and their resolution are, by virtue of that focus, assumed to be their problem and responsibility: a private rather than a collective solution is presupposed, despite the rhetoric of peer-group support. As Dalley noted:

> Much of my research in Scotland had focused on the attitudes of social workers as to where the balance of

responsibility for caring lay between family and state. While many believed strongly that the state had an overriding, collective duty to provide care, a significant proportion believed very firmly in the importance of family responsibility and the overriding necessity of maintaining people at home. It occurred to me that many of these respondents would define themselves as feminists or at least as advocates of the feminist viewpoint. How great, in that case, must the persuasive strength of familist ideology be for such people to give their unquestioned support to the contra-feminist position. (Dalley, 1988: xiii)

For instance, St Michael's, with a strongly woman-validating philosophy, uses family therapy, encounter-type games, counselling, primary care (basic nurture – good food and 'cuddles'), play sessions with children, individual work with children with special needs, health education, literacy and household maintenance. In its leaflet to the general public, St Michael's describes itself as:

> a very special place that tries to enable young children and their parents to gain more from their lives, to reduce the tensions and hardships within their families and to encourage healthy growth and development.
>
> To this end we offer a service that is aimed at both children and their parents, where through structured play, creative learning and family counselling we hope to enrich their lives. (Ely, 1984)

The strong emphasis on self-awareness and personal growth pervades not only the centre's work with the families, but also the staff group. While this is typical of this segment of social work, the psychobabble also has a strategic function in keeping a strong sense of identity and purpose amongst the staff group. This may benefit the project in terms of staff morale, but it does mean that professionals dominate the ethos and methods of the centre – ironically, since the staff also stress the need to demystify professionals' expertise and empower users of services. Users can get this far so long as they conform to the methods and values of the project. The irony of the woman-centred approach is that in practice it becomes woman-targeted: the rhetoric of personal growth and empowerment for women legitimates a practice which is essentially about changing those women's parenting and their domestic behaviour.

Research on users of family centres and other social-work services has highlighted the misunderstandings that occur between client and social worker. Ely (1984) interviewed ten families who attended one of the centres – the Orchard – in my study. They had a range of serious problems – housing, marital, and mental disturbances – but not serious neglect or abuse of their children. Some users had wanted daycare for their children; the fathers found it difficult to attend, expressing considerable ambivalence about the centre. Some feared that their children would learn bad habits; others said that they were bored and did not see the point in watching their child play:

> one client didn't like feeling they had to ask to go out and didn't like the staff around when they were having lunch. One other found it embarrassing when being advised how to handle her child in front of other families.

What is significant is that six families saw the Orchard as a provision *for children* – a kind of nursery. The staff, on the other hand, saw it as a place for teaching and treating *parents*. Asked why they were referred to the Orchard, the families tended to mention problems such as housing, and not to mention marital problems, whereas the reverse was the case when the referring social workers were asked. It is notable that the users did not mind admitting to needing help and advice with childcare problems and their own handling of the children: it was marital problems which were seen as private territory. In Gibbons's (1990) study, many of the parents contacted social services because they wanted help with a child's difficult behaviour, or with some other family relationship problem. In 14 out of 24 cases the social workers saw the problem in the same way as the parents, but:

> Where there was disagreement, the social workers tended to lay more stress on parents' inappropriate methods of discipline or care, rather than to accept the parents' point of view that the children were out of control. (Gibbons, 1990: 133)

This echoes Mayer and Timms's *The Client Speaks* (1970), which showed that clients saw social workers as experts who would tell them what to do for the best, and how to do it. The satisfied clients (and Ely's research showed this too) had social workers who were more supportive-directive than insight-orientated. So at the family centre, Ely's sample appreciated advice on childcare and the willingness to listen to problems, but they resented probing into marital, sexual or family matters, especially in groups. Warren's (1990) sample of users stressed 'straight talking' from family centre staff, and resented a sense of uncertainty about the reason for attendance or evasion about future plans.

In 1984 the London Borough of Camden published research critical of its family centres (then called young family care centres). Probably because of a relatively high degree of autonomy, the centres had developed rather different regimes, ranging from daycare to family therapy. This had produced confusion in the public's mind and resentment because scarcity of places meant that some parents accepted places in centres whose philosophy they disliked. While some mothers appreciated the chance to meet people and get help for themselves at the centres, others said that they resented the imposition of the centre's regime on themselves:

> I'm 33 – lots of other things to do, and I'm sitting in a room playing – why?
> Normal mothers don't spend hours and hours each day playing with their children. (Heiser and Godfrey, 1984: 29)

Mothers who had planned to work resented the involvement expected of them in a family centre. There were also criticisms of basic hygiene and supervision – of the feeling that it is 'more fun to discuss things with kids than change their nappies or wash their faces' (*ibid.*: 30). Some thought the standards of childcare were declining:

> This little girl, she wet herself and the worker was trying to get her to tell her what was wrong at home. I watched it go on for half an hour, was she mad with mummy or what? and she didn't change her pants. (*ibid.*: 29)

Conclusion

Women form the majority of social workers and their clients; the majority of users of family centres are lone mothers (see, for example, Gibbons's study). All the social workers in my study expressed a commitment to the empowerment of women and an awareness of the ways in which welfare can control (through moral judgements tied to rationing, for instance). Yet family centres, in subtle – and not so subtle – ways, controlled and regulated their women users. Since the restraints on welfare expenditure in the 1970s and 1980s it is no longer appropriate to conceive of control as the removal of children from poor families by intrusive social workers. Rather, as Packman found in her research:

> Social workers seem to be developing a practice which says to deprived families that they should be able to care for their children without welfare support and that firm, speedy action will follow if they are not able to provide such care adequately. (Packman, 1981: 127)

As I have stressed, family centres emphasize parental responsibility in their aim of keeping children out of Care, yet keeping families out of the Care system can itself be a form of control. At one end are monitoring and surveillance of families who may be placing their children at risk (Packman *et al.*, 1986), but at the opposite end is the regulation which occurs in the *denial* of support services, so that women have to fall back on their own slender resources – for instance, the vast majority of pre-school provision is in self-help playgroups. In a practical way, then, women are regulated because the lack of support services in the community denies them opportunities and exploits their energies.

Social work and psychoanalysis have always regulated *images* of family life, personal life, and above all of the mother (Donzelot, 1980). I do not propose to go into the vast feminist literature which has demonstrated the patriarchal assumptions and practices in both fields, preferring to take this as read. It is evident from the user studies (e.g. Gordon, 1988) that many women do seek personal help and advice for themselves, but what is also apparent is that the service offered may not be one they would have chosen had they been better informed or more powerful. As it is, mothers in poverty and lone mothers are likely to get a service or treatment which narrowly focuses on themselves as mothers and on their child's well-being, for to offer something more directly for the woman herself would be to condone her 'deviant' family style – even, perhaps, to encourage her to abandon her 'duties'.

Critics of family therapy have noted its reification of the family (Pearson, 1974); its assumption is that families are autonomous units, abstracted from social structures and cultures. Systems theory is silent on the meanings of and differential power in age and gender, assuming that there are common goals and interests in families (Perelberg and Miller, 1990; Poster, 1978). Like psychoanalysis, it has particular implications for women in its strong focus on mothers, often viewing their behaviour and psychopathology as underlying the abuse of or disturbance in a child (Dominelli, 1986), and being inactive in the face of violence against women.

Systems theory denies the world of the unconscious, or the importance of exploring meaning, of attaining insight. It is a masculine form of intervention – goal-orientated, strategic, far from the gentle, listening humanistic therapies. Cohen (1985), discussing the nature of the contemporary 'madness network', suggests that lower-class deviants are more likely to receive social skills training or behaviour modification (of which parentcraft and family therapy are the family centre equivalents), since they are outside the ring of middle-class access to growth and awareness therapies. Yet he notes that there are parts of the community control system where Freudianism and behaviourism blend or are equally available: what the client gets may depend on his or her intelligence, articulacy, sharing of views with therapists, or, on the other hand, cultural distance, impoverished vocabulary, or dangerous behaviour.

At its bleakest, then, we may say that the social work of family centres tends to stress the responsibility of mothers, that it uses therapies – especially family therapy – which are known to be sexist in theory and practice and more focused on behaviour than on meaning, and that it focuses on the mother, helping her only in her role as the mainstay of the family. But I have also shown that all is not negative in family centres: because their roots and philosophies are diverse, there are practices which genuinely empower, offer insight, self-esteem and meaning to individuals, ameliorate the lives of children, and increase the support networks in a community. Within family therapy itself voices are emerging which seek to address power in families and to stress men's responsibilities as well as women's needs. Family centres can, therefore, in my view, regulate and confront behaviour in families in ways which are in children's or women's interests: these will be the focus of my next chapter.

CHAPTER 6

TOWARDS GOOD PRACTICE IN FAMILY CENTRES

In this chapter I aim to show how family centres could (and in some cases do) realize their promise of supporting parents in the care of their children where they are in need, promoting better childcare in families and communities, and empowering their users. That is to say, I shall examine ways in which family centres could promote responsibility and autonomy in parents – not by the deterrent principle which increasingly underlies the British income maintenance and social services systems, but by listening to users' needs, providing services which meet them, and adopting the conclusions of the vast body of research on the relationship between poverty and the quality of family life. It is my intention to review some of this literature to provide a framework which legitimates family centres and social services which link the personal and the political, the private and the public, rather than – as has too often been the case – focusing on the personal without attention to its social, gender, or cultural context.

On this basis, I shall promote the form of family centre which provides, at a local level, a *range of services*, and has features of the neighbourhood, community development or service models of family centres in the way users participate. It is a space for local people to use, the users having in common social need, but otherwise being understood as diverse in terms of age, gender, culture, interests, problems. In so doing I shall refer to a French example of children's and family support. The chapter will review and consider the implications of the recent changes in family structures, then look at the needs of lone parents as users of services. In my research, in that of Gibbons (1990), and others we have reviewed, lone parenthood features prominently amongst users of family centres, yet it is not a form of family which is often valorized in social provision and practice. I will ask whether, and under what circumstances, social work and therapy can empower rather than regulate women. In both this chapter and the next I shall argue that the boundary between private and public needs to be lowered; that it is in both women's and children's interests that it is; and that the severe strain which some families (especially lone parents) currently experience may be exacerbated by government policies which now ask too much of families in the way of responsibility and self-reliance. Public responsibility and collectivism must replace family self-reliance, and be recognized by social workers as worthy and credible aims.

Family diversity: a crisis in 'the' family or a crisis for women?

Are the changes in family life 'disturbing' and the roots of many social problems, as the New Right continues to argue (e.g. Whitfield [1990], at the International Congress for the Family, Brighton), or can we look at change more positively? Certainly there are changes, but what do they mean?

The Commission of the European Communities, in its *Communication on Family Policies* (1989), summarized the changes in family structures and demography across Europe as follows. Since the end of the 1960s there has been a decline in the birth rate in all European countries, and no European Community country, with the exception of Ireland, has achieved full population replacement. This rapid decline has occurred simultaneously in all the countries of Western and Eastern Europe, and affected all strata of society. A parallel trend is an increase in the period of time between marriage and the birth of the first child, and a rise in the number of divorces. There was a 20 per cent decline in the number of marriages between the early 1970s and early 1980s, and:

> an increase in the number of unions 'by agreement' or 'de facto' marriages which would account for the increase in the

> number of children born out of wedlock . . . .With close to
> 40% of births being illegitimate, Denmark occupies an
> entirely exceptional position; the United Kingdom and
> France are in a similar position (roughly 20% in 1985),
> followed by the Federal Republic of Germany, Ireland, the
> Netherlands and Luxembourg, where the rate varies from
> 8%–9% . . . (Commission of the EC 1989: 8)

Illegitimacy is a misnomer, for in a high proportion of cases the
father is registered on the birth certificate, and these unions are
stable cohabitations. However:

> since 1970, there has been a very rapid rise in the divorce
> rate: the number of divorces tripled between 1964 and 1982 .
> ...In the light of the initial data available, the final
> proportion of divorced couples amongst those who married
> in 1975 will probably be over 1 out of 5 in France, over 1 out
> of 4 in England and Wales and close to 1 out of 3 in
> Denmark. (*ibid.*: 8)

There is, then, a new diversity of family models and an
emergence of different types of households, and reconstituted
families. There has been a rapid increase in lone parent families,
usually headed by women:

> while a large part of the population still spends most of its
> life in a so-called 'traditional' (couple with children) family,
> the emergence of other family models raises the question of
> the child's place in an increasingly mobile family context and
> the question of adapting current social legislation to new
> situations. (*ibid.*: 8)

This approach accepts change rather than talking of deviance from
the 'normal'. It recognizes diversity as a feature of society and of
the life cycle: lone parenthood is a stage, and individuals move
through different forms of family and household, rather than
being fixed in a certain type of family. Moss (1988), in his report
for the EC Childcare Network, has also argued that society needs
to respond positively to diversity amongst families with children,
and that especial attention is needed for lone parents, ethnic
minority families, families with disabled children, and rural
families. He confirms that the proportion of lone parents – as a
product of divorce rather than illegitimacy – is increasing in most
EC countries, and that it is highest in Denmark, Germany and the

UK; the UK and Denmark have the highest rates of divorce in the EC. Remarriage and cohabitation with new partners after divorce mean that many children will experience changes in their household composition as they grow up (Moss, 1988: 36).

Kiernan and Wicks's (1990) study confirms these trends in Britain. While noting the continuing stability (78 per cent of British children under 16 live with both natural parents, legally married to each other [1985 figures]), they emphasize that female employment is rising, but that most domestic and caring work inside the family continues to be undertaken by women. They suggest that the impact of the 1992 internal market may be increased labour mobility, with increasing inequalities between regions and increased vulnerabilities for certain groups, especially women.

The EC family policies document also notes the increase in women's employment, partly accounted for by the decline in the birth rate, better access to the labour market, and the consumer society. The biggest growth has been amongst married women between the ages of 25 and 40, and this has occurred both in countries where growth is rapid and in countries where it is slow. Yet part-time, temporary work and homeworking characterize women's employment, in a labour market which is becoming increasingly segregated, diverse and flexible as regards organization of production and labour conditions. It is ethnic minority women and lone parents who are especially vulnerable to these insecurities of the labour market, and who have most difficulty in gaining access to formal and informal sources of good daycare for children.

While access to the labour market may have increased women's opportunities and given them security in the case of divorce or separation, it has also raised issues about reconciling work and family life. We therefore need to understand changes in labour market structures and family structures in terms of the impact they have on each other. These reports argue that family policies must take account of these wider changes and their impact inside families – a point I shall return to in the next chapter, when we consider the status of family and children's policy in Britain.

Given the lack of childcare facilities and an increasingly unregulated labour market in the UK, it seems to me more reasonable to talk of a crisis *for* families, and especially for lone mothers, rather than a crisis *in* the family. It is not changing family structures which cause social problems but the relationship between the family and the state, and policies and practices which the state implements to support or disadvantage certain family forms.

The dynamics of poverty and childcare: a framework for social practice

A primary task for social workers must be to support *families as they exist*, not to become part of a policy which punishes 'deviant' families. A first step can be to see lone mothers' major problem as poverty, and to realize that poverty is a feminist issue. Rather than being seen primarily as needing psychological help for parenting problems, mothers can be seen as needing practical services and as unemployed or seeking work or training. Daycare, providing opportunities for parents and enriching experiences for children, should not be cynically abandoned as an unrealistic objective. This requires a different framework of thinking from that which predominates in some family centres and their managing organizations. Social workers need to escape from the mood of pessimistic determinism which underlay the 'cycle of deprivation' thesis in the mid 1970s, with its focus on parenting behaviour and acceptance that an expansion in daycare services was 'unrealistic', and even damaging to family life.

Critiques of the 'cycle of deprivation' thesis provide some pointers for good practice in family centres. Sir Keith Joseph's speech in 1972 provoked an outcry from academics and the poverty lobby: he seemed to be blaming the poor for their poverty and, like Charles Murray today (1984), to be pointing to an underclass, characterized by 'disorganized' family life, which carries and spreads society's pathologies.

Townsend (1979) criticized the 'cycle of deprivation' as a mixture of popular stereotypes and contentious scientific notions, and a selection of types of deprivation at the expense of others: redundancy, dirty and dangerous working conditions, poor schools and poor housing were ignored; child-rearing practices were held responsible for intellectual and emotional impoverishment and targeted for solutions. Despite the fact that in the United States little support had been found for the theory that poverty rests on intergenerational transmission, the theory helped in the USA to:

> divert interest . . . from economic and social reconstruction to individual training and character reform, from costly redistributive policies to low-cost social work and community psychiatry . . . .(Townsend, 1979: 70)

In 1974 Sir Keith Joseph commissioned the Social Science Research Council to carry out research into the cycle in order that social policies could intervene into deprivation more effectively, 'and perhaps find ways of breaking the cycle' (Joseph, 1974). The research was carried out by academics and professionals from a variety of social scientific backgrounds. They were asked to investigate many aspects of deprivation and their transmission between generations. The research, published as *Studies in Deprivation and Disadvantage*, began appearing in 1976, focusing on health, education, housing, and 'problem family' life, as well as on programmes and policies. Most of the researchers criticized Sir Keith Joseph's term and preferred to use the term 'disadvantage' (a clear lack) rather than 'deprivation', where it is not clear of what the individual or family has been deprived. All found scant support for the view that social problems are concentrated in and transmitted through particular families. In her final overview of the research, Madge (1983) noted that while there could be similarities between parents and their children's styles of coping, family background *on its own* could not predict families at risk. The risk factors had to be combined with continuing damaging influences: overcrowded and impoverished home conditions, limited educational opportunities and encouragement, low status jobs with low pay. This confirms West's (1982) findings on families and delinquency: it was families where there were *continuing* disturbances, combined with adverse childhood experiences and poor parental care, which produced delinquency.

In their review of existing research on intergenerational continuities in parenting behaviour, Rutter and Madge (1976) noted that most studies which showed such links either looked at extreme forms of abnormalities in behaviour or deprivation, or were retrospective. While these studies showed abnormal childhoods in parents with current problems, they did not show what happened to – and what protected – the majority who did not become problem parents despite early adversity, nor whether individuals' behaviour changes over time and what may modify their behaviour.

Noting studies which had indicated that seriously neglectful mothers could change, and that such change occurred where women had a steady and affectionate husband, Rutter, Quinton and Liddle (1983) compared a group of women who had been in Care as children with a group who had not. The 'in Care' families were substantially more disadvantaged in terms of housing and income, and more of the mothers had suffered psychiatric disorders, with nearly half having been in a psychiatric unit (compared with 2 per cent in the comparison group). The cohabitees of the 'in Care' mothers were more socially deviant, over half having been on probation or in prison, almost half showing a personality disorder, and nearly half with a current psychiatric disorder. In short, the mothers who had been in Care showed more parenting problems, but they also suffered more difficult social circumstances. Rutter *et al.* therefore asked, first, whether it was the poor living conditions that affected their current parenting, and second, what factors had enabled a large group of 'in Care' mothers (about a quarter of the sample) subsequently to show normal parenting and psychosocial functioning. Major protective effects came from a supportive spouse, and from adequate living conditions.

The important conclusion for family centres – indeed, the conclusion which those using the ecological approach have taken as central to their work – is that it is *current* stresses in families which may tip the balance between coping and not coping. Many families will be vulnerable because of adverse childhoods, but that does not necessarily predict adult problems – or rather, in order for these vulnerabilities to become pathologies in adulthood, they must be combined with new adversities: isolation, poverty, unemployment, a violent spouse, more than one pre-school child, poor health. Alternatively, those with adverse childhoods can be protected from their consequences by – as Brown and Harris (1978) showed of women and depression – a close supportive relationship or employment. We cannot therefore, talk of a 'problem family' as a type, but need to understand family difficulties much more dynamically. There are stages in the life cycle of all families; some are more demanding than others.

Coffield *et al.*'s (1981) ethnographic study of 'problem' families showed how such families can be locked into their deviance by ostracism, isolation, lack of supportive kin in the broader family, and chronic material problems. They showed how a family in their study moved into 'normality' through helpful relationships with the husband's kin, and by enormous determination and drive. They talk, therefore, not of a cycle of transmitted deprivation, but of disadvantage as a web in which families can become entangled if their particular mix of circumstances and personal qualities are sufficiently adverse.

This web takes force from public attitudes to 'problem families', who may suffer harassment and bullying of children and negative attitudes from officials. Coffield notes the EC survey *The Perception of Poverty in Europe* (1977), which revealed that the British hold particularly harsh attitudes to the poor, blaming them for their circumstances. Social workers' tendency to focus on intrafamililial qualities and childhood experiences reinforces the model which sees the cause as in the families themselves rather than in the dynamic between them and their environment.

The literature on why children come into Care has underpinned the ecological approach in family centres which prevent children coming into Care by offering support to vulnerable families. This literature has shown that overwhelmingly it is the children of the poor who come into Care: in 1976 Holman, for instance, drew attention to the ways in which the poor are undermined in their attempts to lead a 'normal' life:

> Certain children are unequal in that they and their families lack access to resources which are available to the majority. In response, the state has awarded greater emphasis to 'rescue' services which remove children from their environment, rather than to reforms and services which provide the resources to enable more families to stay together. (1976: 1)

He argued that it was not sufficient to see defective parents and relationships in isolation; his theme, rather, is that 'social provision has failed to ensure – for certain families – the kind of environment which encourages attachment, security, continuity and stimulation' (*ibid.*: 4). He referred to Wilson and Herbert's (1978) research, which showed that the dynamics of the decaying city can make 'good parenting' impossible, however much parents want to be 'good parents' and share generally accepted standards of childcare. In that study (discussed in Chapter 4) parents in poor neighbourhoods either tended to give up on normal standards of care and supervision, finding them hard to enforce (and their children were likely to become delinquent), or were very strict with their children, isolating them from the perceived contamination of local 'bad' influences. While these families did protect their children from delinquency, they did so at some cost to them.

Holman's 1976 study showed what has been confirmed since: that children in Care have come overwhelmingly from working-class parents and that children of one-parent families are at special risk – as are those from large families with low incomes, in inadequate housing, and in areas of social deprivation. He noted that poverty can impair parenting capacity through ill health, lack of play facilities, lack of books and toys. Parents' self-esteem may be low and, feeling that they cannot participate in normal social life, they may withdraw into apathy or aggression: the poor are handicapped by their poverty *and* by lack of resources of a general and social kind, which has secondary consequences of low self-esteem and isolation. A study of children entering Care in 1987 (Bebbington and Miles, 1989) found that 50 per cent were living with one adult only, compared with 7 per cent in the general populaton; 75 per cent of the families lived on Income Support, and over 50 per cent in poor neighbourhoods. The study aimed to update the findings of Packman's 1962 study, and found that entry to Care appeared to be even more closely associated with social deprivation than it was in 1962.

Child abuse is also associated with poverty, and it is crucial for good practice in family centres to acknowledge this, for the 'myth of classlessness' can be used by professionals to justify intervention which does not engage with the social needs of abusing families (Pelton, 1978, cited in Parton, 1985). The individualist, psychomedical approach tends to look for key traits of the pathological parent; most of the studies are based on small samples of people who have already been labelled and processed by professionals, without controls for comparison. Researchers 'look for' abnormalities which are then used to construct the individualist model. The result is a jumble of factors and traits which overpredict the incidence of abuse (Gelles, 1979; Sheppard, 1982). Yet many studies have clearly associated child abuse and poverty. Creighton's (1984) study of NSPCC Special Unit Registers of children from 1977 to 1982 noted that earlier studies' findings were replicated, and that unemployment rates were particularly high in both men and women and, indeed, were rising.

Parton (1985: 153) concurs with these NSPCC findings, arguing that 'the highest incidence of the problem occurs in families experiencing the most extreme poverty'. The evidence from the USA is similar – for instance, in Gil's (1970) nationwide survey, which found that child abuse was associated with low income and poor education. He argued that child abuse in the family is a lesser social problem than the institutional and structural factors which impede the development of children: poverty, racial discrimination, poor diet, and inadequate medical care and schooling. The family is an agent in a broader system of provision and deficit in society, which means that lower-class children are more likely to suffer from both familial and social deficits, possibly in a cultural context of a greater readiness to use force and violence. Yet poverty itself cannot be said to cause abuse, because the majority of poor families do not abuse their children. Instead it can be seen, on the one hand, as an indirect cause of abuse, as it represents social policies which sanction the existence of poverty, poor income, bad housing and decaying neighbourhoods in which children live. On the other hand it can, Gil suggests, be seen as a 'triggering context': a source of frustration and stress for adults rearing children. He interrelates psychological stress, poverty, and the culturally sanctioned use of physical force in society with psychopathological states.

In Craig and Glendinning's study (1990), tensions over money damaged family relationships and had either contributed to separations or undermined current relationships, and 'these tensions were sometimes expressed in anger or withdrawal by parents from their children or from each other' (Craig and Glendinning, 1990: 27). Lone parents in Britain suffer poor health when they are in the low social strata: Popay and Jones (1990) reported that from their secondary analysis of the General Household Survey:

> On all measures except long-standing illness the poor health of lone mothers compared to that of lone fathers stands out. They have even higher rates of long-standing illness than fathers in couples. There are considerable gender differences in the socio-economic circumstances of lone parents: lone mothers are less likely to be in employment and to be home-owners than lone fathers. (Popay and Jones, 1990: 530)

This is the background of the families who are 'targeted' by family centres, the families with children in need.

Towards good practice

Such is the framework necessary for empowering practice in family centres. Several factors should be recognized: gender, poverty and unemployment, environmental decay and poor public services, isolation, ill health, psychological vulnerability. None on its own causes family breakdown or child abuse, but the particular mix families experience can make or break them.

Family centres with an ecological approach (usually those other than social-work/child protection centres) have always stressed this framework, seeing themselves as a supportive space which contributes in both practical and psychological ways to a family's resources, offering the possibilities for friendships and networks to grow, thus overcoming isolation. Centres can provide health education and counselling to address psychological vulnerabilities, and provide compensating and enriching experiences for children. At their best, then, family centres do not claim to overcome poverty, or to rid society of child abuse, but they do seek to tip the balance for families whose lives are a severe struggle, and to prevent others becoming trapped in the web of deprivation and dependence (on the state, relatives, or friends).

A French example

The French *centres socio-culturels* which were observed for comparison with English family centres were run by the *Caisse d'Allocations Familiales*, a semi-public body which is the main provider of family and child benefits, and of social welfare services to families. The exact division of responsibility between CAF and the *départemental* (equivalent to local authority) social services department varies: a local contract is made specifying exactly which organization (and there are others) will carry out statutory responsibilities for child protection and infant welfare, as well as the promotive child welfare policies enshrined in French social policy and national plans. CAF's current priorities are: supporting the family, whatever its form, improving services for 0–6 year olds, reaching isolated mothers, and working with young people at risk of unemployment and delinquency.

The centres are impressively modern, well designed and equipped, with plenty of space for their teams of workers and their users. They have *haltes-garderies*: nurseries for children who may be left for up to twenty hours per week, on demand, at a token fee. These complement the crèches which are provided by CAF and/or the municipality for children of working mothers, and the *écoles maternelles* (nursery schools) which the vast majority of children above the age of three attend.

The social workers interviewed in the centres were aware of growing problems of poverty, especially amongst single parents and the young unemployed, and of other problems such as the isolation of second-generation ethnic minority children, or the emotional poverty of some children's lives. While the emphasis was on reaching these groups, there was a prevalent view that the social-work task was to promote harmonious relationships *between* social groups – thus to work with a range of groups, not just with the most deprived or those where poor parenting was the issue. So there was a commitment to making the centres a common space for local users, to stimulating a variety of groups and interests, which would offer possibilities for participation by groups at risk of exclusion.

Social work and social action address different levels of problems in the same centres. There are, for instance, compensatory education and play sessions for children whose lives are seriously deprived because they are often left alone in flats while their parents work in the informal economy. Families under court-ordered supervision meet their social workers at the centres. There are social workers (*assistantes sociales*) with caseloads including child protection work, and there is generally available parent-advice work carried out by *conseilleurs en économie sociale et familiale* (family advisers in all aspects of daily life). There are infant health and welfare clinics which all mothers and children attend. Some centres have *animateurs*, who work on local sociocultural activities: school holiday schemes, neighbourhood fêtes, clubs, knowledge and skill exchanges, adult literacy classes, self-help groups in physical and mental health, with youth work especially promoted by the government to prevent delinquency (King, 1988).

French social workers are working more and more collectively: we hear the same rhetoric about strengthening networks and communities, but the French attitude is that effective participation – the expression of citizenship – means providing services and animating groups which the more fragile can use on the same basis as everyone else (for a fuller discussion, see Cannan *et al.*, 1992). Effective integration (as opposed to marginalization) means that services should strengthen citizens' lives: family and childcare services are investments against deviance or dependence. Mothers are seen as needing practical support as well as time to themselves if they are to be 'good mothers'; and children, as future citizens, are assumed to need good quality public services in their own right. Social workers, therefore, aim first to set up general, non-stigmatizing services and groups, and then to help the 'at risk' use those services as well as to develop informal sources of care.

La Guérinière is a centre on a dreary estate in a northern industrial city. The housing is markedly drab, consisting entirely of cheaply built public housing erected shortly after the wartime destruction. There is high unemployment, and there are many lone-parent families. Next to the centre are the municipal crèche, the nursery school, an old people's day centre, and a leisure and sport centre for young people. Despite the dreary housing, then, there is no shortage of social provision. The CAF centre, like the others, has gradually moved from individual casework to collective ways of working. The project has a compensatory scheme for 3- and 4-year olds who tend to be left alone in their flats; the social workers originally aimed to involve the mothers, but they just wanted to leave the children and take some time for themselves. Now this need is recognized as legitimate, though the workers continue to devise activities and outings which might attract or interest parents, who are mainly single mothers, with low self-esteem and little confidence. As in the other centres, it is hoped that the mothers will raise their standards of care by becoming familiar with good practice as observed in the centre, but they are not coerced into participation.

At this centre the *halte-garderie* was making particular efforts to respond to local needs and patterns of life – recognizing, for instance, the late rising hours of both adults and children, and therefore considering evening sessions (acknowledging mothers' needs to go out in the evening, the need to provide a safe baby-sitting service). There were imaginative ideas about the design of the centre: a new reception area drew parents through the *halte-garderie*, so that they could see more of it and its ideas of play and childcare, rather than, as before, just leaving children at the door.

Service and opportunity models in the UK

This model, seen in the French example, is also found in some of the English family centres cited in this study – for instance the Elm (described in Chapter 2) – although not all lived up to the model, for reasons I shall discuss. St John's (see Chapter 2), and the Defoe Day Care Centre in the London Borough of Hackney (established as part of the European Poverty Programme in 1974), both attempt to alter local opportunity structures. Defoe's initial objective in 1976 was to:

> offer an opportunity to parents to combat poverty through further education and an opportunity to combat the disadvantage associated with poverty by furthering their understanding of the total needs of their children, and through this to develop a wide range of supporting links within the racially-mixed community.

As a long-term aim, it set out to 'help prevent the babies of young unsupported mothers being taken into local authority care'

(Willmott and Mayne, 1983: 19–20). The centre had a policy of offering daycare so that women could work, and of employing local people, so that its overall effect was to change the material situation for local families as well as benefiting the children.

The London boroughs with Labour-controlled councils and strong equal opportunities policies also ran centres which combined *services* with activities aimed at empowering users and altering the balance of their lives (described by Walker [1991] as the direct service model). In Lambeth, for instance, daycare was not seen just as 'an opportunity to convey the skills of parenting' (Parker, 1980) but as a service which ranges from:

> non-accidental injury, where intensive work is needed to care for both child and family. In other families, the most effective way of preventing family breakdown through the experience of stress or grinding poverty may be to offer daycare as an opportunity for the parent to gain independence from state benefits. (Dennis and Wallis, 1982: 43)

In my view, the most effective family centres offer a range of services and resources for families, and these are provided in the spirit of acknowledging that families – and especially lone mothers – need services and formal and informal resources if the parents are to succeed as (and to enjoy being) parents. These services should range from daycare to enable women to work or play sessions for the benefit of children, to spaces for self-help and user groups, to health care, adult education, counselling and therapy. User surveys have shown that this is what the public want and appreciate. In 1988 the Social Services Inspectorate reviewed statutory family centres and found that the successful centres had an open-door policy, were well known by local communities, used local staff and volunteers, and did not make their users feel stigmatized or inadequate. Stones (1989) carried out an assessment of local need before the opening of a Barnardo's centre in Bristol. The 100 families consulted had nothing good to say about their estate, but wanted safe play areas and other facilities for children. They suffered isolation and regretted the absence of community feeling as experienced in burglaries and vandalism. Isolation from wider families was an issue for 43 per cent of the families interviewed. Gibbons (1990) discovered that parents found daycare and playgroups invaluable.

and that those who used any kind of daycare showed more improvement in parenting than those with other forms of help.

Offering daycare and other services to children is an approach that is regaining some ground – Manchester City Council, for instance, has recently opened children's centres which offer daycare places, after-school facilities, and space and resources for informal parent and toddler groups (Cohen and Fraser, 1991). The frank acknowledgement that daycare is good for children, a depathologizing of the service, is needed so that it can lose its stigma and empower its users (Frost and Stein, 1989). We will return to daycare debates in the next chapter.

Research on playgroups is relevant to family centres which involve parents in an exploitative fashion (self-help rather than service provision). Ferri and Niblett (1977) found that in playgroups in deprived areas the notion of involving mothers under strain in help rotas and social activities was unworkable. Those playgroups which did retain contact with such mothers were those whose:

> first priority was often relief from the responsibility of caring for children for a couple of hours, rather than the extra commitment of involvement in the playgroup's activities. In this situation, many of the groups in the study saw a need to provide something *for* mothers rather than expect a contribution *from* them. In most cases this simply meant offering a welcoming atmosphere, a place to sit down and relax, having a cup of tea and talking over problems with other mothers or with the playgroup staff . . . . (Ferri and Niblett, 1977: 12)

This is an important point of comparison with family centres, some of which try to provide a welcoming, supportive yet undemanding space for mothers in order to encourage them to use the facilities and to give them respite, and the beginnings of a network. Centres which involve mothers in more structured activities do not always check that they are willing and able to participate: as Ely (1984) found, there can be resentment and misunderstanding. It is important, then, to provide a welcoming but undemanding space for mothers as something for themselves. But they may not wish to participate in the work of the centre, even if they feel strong: Finch's research on mothers and playgroups in deprived areas found that what the mothers most desired was a quality, professional service for their children, and they did not see themselves or women like themselves as able to provide it (Finch, 1984).

Social workers are *sympathetic* to these needs of their clients, and aware of issues of poverty, discrimination, and gender. But their practice in family centres does not always reflect that sympathy. Why?

Gender, participation, empowerment

The direction which family centres have taken is very much a consequence of the enterprise of social workers who are interested in family therapy. Those which developed from nurseries have shifted their focus from children and their needs; social services departments anxious about child abuse accepted the family therapists' claims that this was an effective form of intervention and treatment. With its ethos of responsibility, it was also a form of intervention which meshed with concerns to reduce dependence on social welfare. It was gender- and culture-blind, and did not ask awkward questions about daycare and other service needs of poor parents.

Family therapy may be an appropriate choice for certain families at certain times. But in family centres it should be part of a *range* of services and methods of helping, so that the centre does not become a closed clinical and stigmatized setting – an institution far removed from the general preventive aims of supporting families in need. All research shows how such families welcome basic services, space, respite, daycare and playgroups, welfare rights, low-key counselling and group-work, holiday schemes, etc. They have not, as so many social workers have assumed, seen 'Care' as necessarily a bad thing (Packman, 1981; Packman *et al.*, 1986), and many families have survived by using the Care system for respite: the Care system and family centres, then, should be highly permeable: there should not be high boundaries between centres and the public, or the 'in Care' and 'not in Care' status. This is what the 1989 Children Act promises, but whether it can be successful will depend largely on resources: will local authorities be able to fund a generous and adequate system of respite care and support services?

But it also depends on social workers, for it has been their highly critical views of the Care system, as well as their desire to distance themselves from the practical work of daycare and support to families and to move into the prestigious world of family therapy that have pushed many family centres away from the general needs of poor families. As Jordan says:

> there isn't much professional kudos in work which is essentially low key, pragmatic, often practical and quite humble, and where power is shared very equally, not merely with other professionals, volunteers and lay people but also with the clients themselves. (Jordan, 1987/8: 9)

Family centres need to offer *space* to women and to children. The unfortunate implication of the term *family centre* (as uncovered by looking at its history in Chapters 3 and 4) is that of the family as a single, homogeneous whole – a view compounded by family therapy, which sees the individuals in a family as having meaning in terms of the family system. But members of families have *different interests* and needs: children need safe and imaginative play space and social activities, respite from difficult home conditions and compensatory play and care, and protection and therapy if they have been abused. Women using family centres may be lone parents on benefit living in depressing estates, may lack self-esteem and need respite from the daily grind, acceptance of themselves. They may want a space which offers possibilities and opportunities ranging from creative activities, welfare rights advice, health education, counselling and therapy, and daycare if they are seeking employment or training.

Men tend not to use family centres to the degree that women do, though in the child protection centres they may be required to attend if parenting is in question. To some extent they come to centres' 'masculine' activities like youth clubs, unemployed clubs, DIY clubs, etc. There is a grey area where men's needs are neglected, yet where men are not held responsible for family life as women are – for it is the women who are encouraged to attend. Family centres should extend and legitimate men's caring roles, providing spaces for non-custodial fathers to be with their children, and counselling with a focus on relationship issues, or on unemployment and training. Where children are at risk or have been abused, perpetrators should be held responsible rather than women blamed for failure to protect children.

Participation, partnership and involvement, let alone empowerment, are terms used loosely in family centres, with the possibilities of resentment and confusion we referred to above. It is important that family centres get clear, and make clear to users, what kind of user involvement they are proposing, and what its boundaries might be. For family centres – as opposed, say, to community centres or a centre for people with disabilities – there may be different kinds of involvement and different power relations between users and workers, according to their reason for using the centre.

The current vogue for participation has two roots, based on two traditions, which can cause confusion in practice. Croft and Beresford (1990) distinguish, first, *consumerism*: this approach tends to be service-provider-led. It is based on marketing principles, on giving the customer more rights and more say in the goods 'purchased'. Recently it has been introduced into the public services, for instance in *Caring for People: Community care in the next decade and beyond* (DOH, 1989), and in the Citizen's Charters both main political parties released in 1991. The assumption is that with more consumer control (and less professional dominance) services will become more effective, efficient and competitive. The second is *self-advocacy*: here the approach is user-led, by users interested in empowerment and control of services. It grows from the international disability and mental health movements, and from the self-advocacy movements of people with learning difficulties from the 1970s onwards.

The consumerist approach to involvement means that agencies seek information from users so that they can provide more sensitive services: 'consultation' is the most appropriate term for this kind of involvement. The self advocacy approach is one where people want a direct say in how services that concern them should be run, perhaps to the extent of wanting delegated powers to run them themselves. Croft and Beresford (1990) suggest that social service organizations clarify the kind of participation, and the purposes of this involvement they are proposing to their publics. Is consultation about what services people want a one-off exercise or a process of participation? Do users want participation (is it a burden, an exploitation of them, as in some playgroups) or would they prefer professionally administered services? What are the ground rules and limits of participation? – we have seen that in some family centres users have tried to exclude some groups and families and resist anti-racism (e.g. Stones, 1989). Is the involvement from choice, or from a kind of compulsion, as with families whose parental rights may be at risk?

Croft and Beresford's findings and principles of good practice are based on a national survey of user and local involvement in social services. They found that a commitment to involvement was widespread in both statutory and voluntary sectors (indeed, it was in some traditional voluntary agencies that there was greatest resistance to the principle, because the organization was based on doing *for* rather than *with* certain groups – 'the' handicapped, 'the' aged, etc.). Yet genuine partnership was also problematic, something being struggled with in practice. At one extreme it meant giving individuals a greater say in their own cases – for instance through complaints procedures, access to records, parental and/or child participation in case conferences and reviews. At the other end were agency initiatives to hear the views of groups of users, and advocacy schemes to help people have more say in agencies. There are problems in the latter model in terms of how far, for instance, residents' committees can actually control the running of an elderly people's or disabled people's home, given organizational constraints on staffing, budgets, and so forth; even so, some organizations take such involvement further than others, and some are clearer than others about what the consultation or involvement is for.

Within social work there are attempts to make practice more participatory and empowering. Feminist approaches stress a partnership between worker and client, the similarity of women's experience if both are female, despite class differences. In family therapy, as in psychotherapy and counselling, feminist approaches are being aired. These stress 'the personal is political' and affirm women's experience rather than problematizing it; they attempt to make the client–therapist relationship as egalitarian as possible by demystifying the therapy and explaining the processes and interpretations, and by offering more self-disclosure than is traditional in psychoanalytic models. Sexual stereotyping is checked, and strategies of intervention are considered in their gender assumptions: is problem-solving a more masculine mode, the processing of experience a more feminine one? Are women disadvantaged by the former, men by the latter? Is the stance of neutrality in family therapy actually a mask for negating women's experience and approach; should feminist therapists be *less* neutral, recognizing the vulnerability of the women they are working with and explicitly aiming to develop their independence and self-esteem, redressing the power imbalance in the family (Perelberg and Miller, 1990)?

Hanmer and Statham (1988: 140–43)) advocate a code of practice in social work which involves both personal awareness of gender issues amongst women and men in agencies, and active practices designed to overcome discrimination. This code of practice is based on the principle of believing and validating women clients, supporting them in such a way that both commonalities and diversities in women's experience can be recognized and learnt from. They advocate collective, non-hierarchical ways of working, aimed at the sharing of experience, resources, and methods of coping. They recommend ways of working with women which create spaces for them in which their sense of control and resistance can be encouraged, and their strengths recognized. Even when 'the news is bad' there should be openness and honesty – something that is also stressed by parents in Warren's (1990) research on family centres: parents felt particularly mistrustful and resentful when they suspected that daycare or similar services were offered for monitoring or assessment purposes rather than as a direct benefit. Hanmer and Statham point to the need for clarity about accountability and the extent of power each party has. Social workers, they say, should work to increase the resources for women, and work with or refer women to agencies which offer empowering experiences: Women's Aid, Rape Crisis, Incest Survivors' Groups, Black Women's Groups.

Conclusion

These principles preoccupied many of the social workers in my study, but in my view family centres cannot become genuine supports to families in need (however 'empowering' the theory) if they concentrate only on treatment, parentcraft and monitoring approaches with families referred by social workers because of parenting problems. These approaches must be combined with services and opportunities, and social workers need to broaden their goals: not just improved parenting behaviour, reduced use of care services, less child abuse, but greater opportunities for women, enriched lives for children through play schemes and daycare, which in their own way can reduce the stresses in families. The so-called crisis in the family cannot be resolved by therapy alone. Nor can it be resolved by seeing the family as a homogeneous unit: its members have different needs and interests at different times in the family life cycle: family centres can support families more by recognizing their varied needs and responding to their choices rather than by regulating them as a single system. But because the more hidden agenda of family centres is to promote independence from the welfare state, they are necessarily restrictive in their services and are people-changing rather than service organizations.

Participation can be genuine only if there is a range of services and opportunities to participate in: otherwise, we are talking only of involvement and supervision of particular families. Social workers in this and other studies, while focusing their practice on family behaviour, nevertheless acknowledge the need for more resources for the families they saw as suffering above all from poverty. All this points to the ecological approach and to the neighbourhood, community development and service models, with a range of services and a space which can be used as an extension of the family – reducing the family's privacy, yet also increasing its strength.

In my next and final chapter I shall turn to the social policy implications: can the state promote equal opportunities *and* support the family? Why are these aims seemingly incompatible in Britain but not in continental Europe? Don't we need public childcare which recognizes family responsibilities as a continuing part of women's lives, but also promotes men's participation in such responsibilities? Women should not just be 'freed' to compete in the male labour market; they need some special treatment to enable them, without stress, to reconcile domestic and work responsibilities. Children need to be seen as society's responsibility and a social resource, not left to individual parents to manage as best they can. Parents should not be 'made' to be responsible by coercive or harsh policies, but supported in a variety of ways and in diverse forms of household. Childcare and family services should be accessible, flexible, and offer a range of choices. These things should not be seen as 'too expensive' but as investments in the quality of society and in the quality of children's lives. It is crucial that social workers do not lose sight of these principles in their practice.

CHAPTER 7

NEW FAMILY POLICIES

This book has been a case study of the processes of change in the welfare state in the UK. It has been argued that the new welfare pluralism has had a particular impact on women, who are already given very little state support in their caring tasks, whether for children, elderly or disabled people – the shift to pluralism has underlined informal and voluntary care rather than state, collective provision. Services are increasingly targeted and problem-orientated. The promotion of the private sector for those who can pay for services has meant that childcare and family services are characterized by inequity and lack of choice and autonomy for their users. At the same time, low levels of community care provision, minimal social security benefits, and the run-down of institutional psychiatric provision appear to have increased the level and intensity of demand on social workers and services such as family centres.

I have been at pains to show that the inequity in childcare and the crisis for (rather than in) poor families, and especially for lone parents, have not been entirely initiated by the New Right: it is more that the Conservatives have worsened divisions in society. There is a long tradition of British individualism which opposes the family and the state, and limits state intervention to families with pathologies: delinquency, educational disadvantage, child abuse. Family centres are neither a simple reflection of government (New Right) policy of the 1980s, nor of the Labour Party/social democratic policies and pressure groups of the 1970s from which debates on the childcare system, the Children Act and family centres originally emerged. The New Right created an

ideological *context*, focused aroun
transmitted deviance, and welfare
establishment (itself internally diverse) co
the childcare debate: the more critical voice
lobby, the organizations calling for better da
the women's aid movement, were marginalized b
lishment. Parental responsibility became a unifying
meaning, on closer inspection, different things to dif
organizations and individuals; hence the underlying confusion a
contradictions in family centre aims and in the issue of user
participation. Voluntary organizations needed to strengthen their
place in the welfare state and were attracted by the shift to
preventive, community-based services. The social-work profession and social services departments, under pressure from rising
demand and expenditure restrictions, sought to influence developments in family services, in pluralism and in decentralization.
At the front line social workers have struggled to shape the
centres in which they work and the local policies of which they
are part.

Family centres, then, reflect not the triumph of certain ideas
but a fluid area of political bargaining, at which local as well as
national struggle is important. The outcome is variability and
diversity: while we can, as this book shows, discern trends and
directions in family centres, the centres themselves are not
identical, and the workers within them are highly conscious of
their actions in shaping and debating aims and practices. While
the New Right and the state determine the broad parameters of
policy, there is considerable local manoeuvring and influence, if
not autonomy. So this has not been a book about whether family
centres 'work', for in uncovering their roots we see that we have
to ask 'for whom, and how, and in what way do they work?' When
we discussed the models which social workers have used for
understanding family centres, they were criticized for paying too
little attention (by ignoring gender issues) to the deeper aims and
functions of these centres. To the social work/child protection
(client-centred), neighbourhood, and community development
models I added the service model, for it seemed to me that the
debate had shifted so far that universal child-centred childcare
services which also promote equal opportunities are no longer
seen as credible objectives for the social services. The aim of this

...hould be – partly by
...d partly by consider-
...shall contrast to the
...d by discretionary ser-

...e policies

...m day nurseries and from
...are almost universally pre-
...essive and innovative, it is my
...need to be cautious in our
welco... ...t the demise of public daycare
in Britain, an... ...the social work profession and
the voluntary childcare ... ...s into a narrow welfare service
focused on those defined as not coping or seriously disadvantaged
– to the discomfort of many who are 'only' poor. As I have
shown, both social workers and voluntary organizations have
been eager to move in this direction – the first group because it
provided a resource for 'dangerous' families which also enabled
social workers to specialize in family therapy; the second because
of their increasing role in a welfare state now characterized by
welfare pluralism. Where community work has been part of
childcare initiatives, its effect, while emphasizing poverty and the
failure of government adequately to house or provide decent
living standards for many families, has been to engineer increasing exploitation of the informal sector in childcare – mothers
themselves.

Day nursery places in the public sector are now at less than half
their 1945 levels; private nurseries, by contrast, expanded by 44
per cent between 1985 and 1988 (Moss, 1991). We see, in the
decline of public day nurseries and the growth of family centres,
the changing balance between the four welfare sectors: the
private, the informal, the statutory, and the voluntary. In Britain
the relationship between the family and the state which was
drawn in the 1940s establishment of the welfare state may have
been a strange interlude in the history of British social policy: as
Finch suggests:

That analysis would further support the view that the prospects for successfully redrawing the boundaries between the state and the family in the provision of welfare are quite rosy since the change in beliefs and values which needs to be engineered is merely a re-assertion of values and ideas which have strong historical roots in British cultural life, even if they have been somewhat obscured and overlaid by naive socialist ideas prevalent in the post-war period. (Finch, 1989: 163)

The long history of British individualism and libertarianism has produced attitudes to state intervention in 'private' life which are increasingly divergent from those in some other European countries. In the UK the conditions of the Second World War produced a brief flowering of collectivism and a democratization of services, a flowering which has since withered under both Labour and Conservative governments. The New Right has built on traditional and patriarchal Fabian/social democratic ideology, particularly that concerning family life – an ideology which had itself moved rightwards in its advocacy of welfare pluralism and targeting in the 1970s (Beresford and Croft, 1984). The mini-malism in the 1989 Children Act (only families in need require state support, the normal family is independent of and private from the state) had all-party support in the Act's passage through Parliament.

Moss (1991) has summed up British ideology as one which asserts that mothers of pre-school children should be at home and that separation of mothers from children in daycare is harmful. Fathers should work full-time, taking responsibility for their family, though they should share in some of the domestic tasks and be present at the births of their children. The New Right (and probably much of the middle ground) sees the decision to have children as a private matter: responsible parents make a decision which should take into account their financial commitment. The state should intervene only in the cases of those who present a risk to themselves or society. If mothers wish to work, that is their choice, and they can purchase the necessary care in the market. In contrast, in France children are viewed as future citizens and as members of the fundamental social institution, the family; they therefore all have a right to state services (Baker, 1986).

The dangers of separation of mother and young child were widely disseminated at the end of the war in, for instance, Winnicott's radio broadcasts, in magazines and in childcare books. This history and its consequences for women have been well documented. Even the war nurseries, which had extolled the benefits of daycare to children as well as to working mothers, were actually limited to 'childcare *while* and *where* women's labour was needed' (Riley, 1983: 137). While the post-war labour shortages meant that in certain areas and industries daycare continued, there was no all-round increase:

> No broadly emancipating moves towards what the Trades Union Council had used to call the 'social recognition' of childcare accompanied the cries for female labour. Nurseries, the business more and more of private employers, were increasingly tied in with the fluctuating needs of those employers, and less and less to any conception of social need. (*ibid.*)

Instead, the post-war rhetoric was natalistic and familist. Neither the TUC nor the Labour Party argued for improved or extended daycare. Women who went out to work were criticized as shameful: Riley describes *Picture Post* articles in which heartless mothers were portrayed leaving miserable children in dismal nurseries: 'Is it *really* necessary in this Welfare State for women to go out to work, or do they do it for the ice cream and the TV?' (*ibid.*). The post-war movement to promote the family was concerned less with services to families in general than with opening up and correcting certain kinds of families. What family policies there were, though ungendered, were targeted on the mother, especially the problem or feckless mother. Both Conservatives and Fabians saw nurseries as places where mothers would learn about nutrition and hygiene as well as receiving help and respite in their task of rearing a large family: domestic strains must be reduced; the burden of child-rearing (for these families only) must be shared.

The social-work profession expanded: childcare officers established by the 1948 Children Act would work with less capable mothers, using nurseries and children's homes as resources. The child psychology of the time, which formed the conventional wisdom of social workers – that of Bowlby and Winnicott –

stressed the preeminence of the mother–child bond. Fathers were invisible, or necessary only as models of authority and masculinity. Failure of family life and separation of children from their mother were assumed to underlie delinquency and maladjustment, and – as we saw in Chapter 4 – delinquency prevention meant family casework.

As we saw in Chapter 3, educational disadvantage was a strong theme in the 1970s, especially under Labour and within Fabian and social democratic circles. Nursery education was set to expand – indeed, it was when Margaret Thatcher was Minister of Education that the White Paper *Education: A framework for expansion* (DES, 1972) was produced. Nursery education would complement the mother's care, being for only short hours each day, and would draw mothers into schools, for instance in helping children to read. The Plowden Report (1967) and the conference on 'Educational Disadvantage' in 1975 (DES, 1975) stressed adult education – education of mothers in childcare and pedagogy – in overcoming class differences in attainment. The DHSS/DES conference on 'Low Cost Day Provision for the Under Fives' (DHSS/DES, 1976) says it all in its title: self-help playgroups rather than publicly subsidized daycare were to be the way forward, especially in the then fashionable aim of breaking the 'cycle of deprivation'– intervening in poor parenting to reduce delinquency and school failure.

The childcare issue since the mid 1970s has been child abuse. A consequence of media and professional fascination with child abuse is that the drive of the childcare services has shifted to procedures and technologies for detecting and protecting children in danger. While it is right that child abuse is acknowledged and acted on, in Britain the effects of this advance have been paradoxical: a deterioration of and a decline in the general services for children, as well as the Care system. Rather than attempting to improve the day nurseries and children's homes, both left libertarian social and community workers and traditionalists in the voluntary organizations have denigrated the existing Care system (Packman, 1981; Packman *et al.*, 1986). Despite a history of excellence in certain sectors of the residential childcare field, and despite the fact that young people sometimes prefer a residential to a foster home, residential children's homes have had an increasingly bad press (Frost and

Stein, 1989: 114–15). The causes of child abuse have been seen as lying in the family *and* in the Care system – as in the 'cycle of deprivation', whereby it was assumed that poor parents were the products of adverse childhoods, including periods in Care. The solutions have been to push care back on to families, as in the 1989 Chidren Act, and to restrict or reduce day and residential care rather than improving and extending them, and opening families' access to them. Yet the evidence is that daycare may be the most effective way of supporting families: Gibbons's (1990) research on family projects in two areas found that any form of daycare provision was strongly associated with amelioration of parenting problems.

Melhuish and Moss (1991) note that in most European countries the former welfare emphasis in daycare has given way to more open access since the 1970s. Accompanying this is a shift from a health-and-welfare framework to an educational/peda-gogical approach stressing the social benefits of daycare for all children. This has tended to raise the status of nurseries and their workers, especially in Sweden and France. The expansion in numbers of places and in the types of children attending mean that children of professonal and middle-class parents use public nurseries: there is relative equity in access and social mixing rather than the concentration of deprived and disturbed children that is found in public nurseries in the UK.

There have been attempts in the UK to move day nurseries from their social-work focus to a more educational model. The period of innovation in education following the Plowden Report in 1967 and the subsequent Educational Priority Areas experi-ment led to a dissatisfaction with the distinction between pre-school *care* (day nurseries) and *education* (nursery classes). If education were to be a means of tackling disadvantage, the concentration of 'priority' children in day nurseries was a questionable practice. Plowden (1967) had referred to the nursery class as 'an outpost of adult education if it is to attain its goal for young children'. The National Children's Bureau evaluated the work of seven nursery centres in 1975 (Ferri *et al.*, 1981). These combined care and education with a policy of parental involvement. While the staff endorsed the principle, parents' presence in the nursery itself caused apprehension, with some staff showing markedly hostile attitudes towards the parents. The nursery nurses were more hostile towards the parents than the teachers, and many considered that the parents were taking advantage of the nursery, using it as a convenient dumping ground and generally having things made too easy for them. These staff attitudes were partly related to training, but were underscored by methods of allocating places. The 'priority' children were perceived differently by the staff. Welfare services were regarded as second best, unlike education, which is a general service.

Within social work, a generally pessimistic air pervaded the research on daycare into the 1980s: there was an assumption that it damaged children, though no hard evidence for this was found (Melhuish and Moss, 1991). The view that nursery care damaged children by separating them from their mothers, and thus undermining their healthy emotional development, underlay or legitimated the shift to maternal involvement in daycare. But pessimistic views of day nurseries, combined with criticism of nursery nurses' attitudes to parents and lack of training in the socioemotional needs of children, were also used to justify their demise (little argument was put forward for improving or extending training). Marshall, for instance, looking at the day nurseries in the London Borough of Camden around 1980, acknowledged that while daycare *could* 'work' for infants, generally the picture was depressing: she observed distressed and often uncomforted infants cared for by the timetable rather than their needs. The nursery nurses had negative views of parents, tending to think that they were having their own needs met rather than their children's, and that they would use the nursery to evade their responsibilities at home or to avoid 'standing on their own two feet' (Marshall, 1982).

So in the late 1970s many day nurseries and children's homes began changing into family centres. This targeting on familial *problems* goes against the trend in Europe, where the educational, social and emotional benefits of a range of childcare services have been stressed. Children and parents of all social classes are seen as needing services, provided in a context of community (and, indeed, national) development.

Contrasting European attitudes: the socially responsible state

The end of the 1980s administration led by Margaret Thatcher was marked by conflict in 1989–90 over attitudes to the European Community and to the vision of Social Europe promoted by Jacques Delors, President of the European Commission. He had sought to open debate on new means of preventing the exclusion of vulnerable sectors of the population – the cost of economic growth – and promoting social cohesion. He drew on a notion of *societal* policies here (those concerned with the big aims of European union and the direction of identity and culture) as opposed to the more detailed social protection measures of *social* policy (Cannan *et al.*, 1992; Vandamme, 1985).

In accordance with its view that growth depends on deregulation in labour markets and employment, the British Conservative government took a minimalist attitude to implementing EC Directives on Equal Pay (1975) and Equal Treatment, and refused to ratify the draft Directives (1983) on leave for family reasons. The European Court of Justice has monitored and furthered equal opportunities legislation, and has dealt with more cases from the UK than from any other EC country (Brewster and Teague, 1989). In 1990 the conflict between the UK and the EC centred on the Community Charter of Fundamental Social Rights of Workers – the 'Social Charter'. The Charter was adopted by eleven of the twelve member states in 1989, and represents the culmination, with the action programme for its implemention, of the European Commission's decision to push ahead with the implementation of the internal market, stressing both economic and social development. The Charter places a responsibility on member states to guarantee social rights, which include protection for part-time and temporary workers and for pregnant women, health and safety regulations, rights to 'decent' wages and minimum incomes, worker participation in management, and rights to training. It states the necessity for measures to combat discrimination in every form, though some British poverty lobby commentators have been suspicious, dismissing the Charter as workerist, arguing that it favours the employed over the poor, the middle-aged over the old, and those with stable employment (e.g. Townsend, 1990).

EC social policy (which owes much to 1980s French socialist policy under François Mitterrand) recognizes that social policy cannot be seen merely as a corrective to economic policy but is a form of action on society which aims to promote growth and employment. The prevention of marginalization and exclusion (for those in declining industries and agricultural regions, and for disabled, ethnic minority and young people, and women) are as important for society as a whole as the promotion of growth. It combines a certain economic liberalism with social protection and human and democratic rights. European conservatives – other than the extremists and the New Right – share many of the principles of social responsibility and social protection with social democrats. Much Christian Democratic thinking draws on Catholic teaching, in which mutual responsibility between individual and society is stressed. The socially responsible state is balanced and complemented by personal responsibility to family and community. Family policies, support services to families in their tasks of caring for children, are a buttress to society because the family is viewed as the basic social institution, the smallest group in society, upon which others rest.

The recent Communication from the Commission of the EC on Family Policies notes the twin changes – in labour markets and in family structures – and argues:

> while the family is the place for the creation of new generations and for initial education, it is also part of the economic sector, for it raises future producers and is a unit of consumption. It also depends on social protection because it receives benefits, it affects women's employment since the woman is generally the member of the couple who brings up the children and cares for the elderly and also pursues an occupation. The family is linked to the environment and to education. As children are becoming more rare, the demographic future of Europe rests with the family. In conclusion the family assumes essential role and place [sic] in the cohesion and the future of society. Therefore it should be protected and specific measures adopted in recognition of the services it renders society. (Commission of the EC, 1989: 12)

These rather natalistic policies echo the brief collectivization of family and children's services in the UK during the 1940s. The distinguishing features of the continental European attitudes are that they accompany a high general level of social protective services, and they accommodate to change in the family rather than seeking to blame family 'deviance' and change for social problems. The family is part of a continuum of social institutions linking individual and society, rather than opposed to and private and separate from the state.

The subsidiarity principle, which evolves from the principles of individualism (self-reliance, personal dignity) and solidarity (mutual bonds within society), promotes and regulates the type of welfare pluralism found in Germany, France and the Netherlands. The state must encourage the preconditions for the emergence of small organizations and for participation in them. This means that the state subsidizes and sponsors independent organizations which are contracted to provide quality services, rather than cheap alternatives:

> Just as individuals should not be prevented from performing their proper functions and responsibilities, by a transfer of these to the community, so higher bodies (including the state) should not take over functions which can be adequately carried out by lower and smaller bodies . . . Subsidiarity goes hand in hand with the primary responsibility attributed to the state to reform the social order, and so acts as a limiting principle giving a proper place to other entities. (Coote, 1989: 157)

Subsidiarity combined with solidarity implies identification with and respect for others, a commitment to the *common* good and to creating bonds between groups, between strong and weak. Solidarity can be expressed between generations – for instance in pension schemes, but also in services for children: those who are adults today will need healthy and productive workers when they are elderly. Finally, it implies what is called social integration, altruism, or 'community' in Britain, and is the root of the contemporary French concern with social integration [*insertion sociale*] (Spicker, 1991).

The EC poverty programmes and social action programmes are based on this social philosophy. Started in 1975, they are action–research programmes which use community work and community development methods and principles of participation by the target populations, and partnership between statutory and voluntary agencies, with the aim of developing better anti-poverty strategies in member states. The poor are viewed as those who are economically and socially excluded, on the fringes of the labour market and social and political life; the projects are expected to devise means of drawing them back into the mainstream (Dennett *et al.*, 1982). Despite economic growth rates of around 3 per cent, proportions of the population on social assistance or in precarious employment appear to be rising in member states. The first poverty programme had estimated that approximately 38 million people were in poverty in member states, while the interim report on the second programme estimated 44 million in 1985 (Room *et al.*, 1989).

The third poverty programme (launched in 1989) focuses on the articulation between economic and social integration of the least privileged groups. The philosophy is that merely giving the poor money will not tackle the issue of 'precariousness': the poor need the means to overcome their poverty – means which include good housing, good health and food, medical care, education, urban renewal, leisure and cultural facilities, a healthy environment, and access to and protection in the labour market. Only when these are tackled together will the cycles of marginalization and exclusion be broken. This EC policy thus has an ultimate, *societal* goal: the promotion of integration and effective citizenship as part of the ultimate goal of solidarity. Social policy is much more than meeting individual need. Because threats to solidarity (caused by the marginalization of certain groups or family vulnerability) are viewed with alarm, the social-work task is – much more than in the UK – one of promoting integration and links *between* social groups rather than targeting services on groups at special risk. The excluded are understood as needing means of participating in society and its public services and institutions in order to make citizenship effective and society cohesive.

Citizenship, women and family services

Citizenship rights consist of political, legal and social rights. Both Left and Right in the UK tend to argue in individualistic terms (for instance in the Labour Party's and the Conservative Party's Citizen's Charters of 1991), and there has been little sense of group rights and social action in social policy, of collective responsibility. Family centres and the policies of which they are a part raise issues of collective provision and relations between groups in their attempt to alter the local ecology and encourage participation within it. But they have little hope of achieving real change without a radical reform of social and environmental services, especially those for children, and without a connection to labour markets and local opportunity structures.

Citizenship rights may be endowed by the state, but there must be certain social and economic conditions which make them effective. Poverty undermines the exercise of citizenship, and poverty is underscored by divisions of race, class, gender, age, disability and employment status (Lister, 1990). There must be social rights *for* citizenship; economic exclusion undermines rights to participate, to be creatively or autonomously involved in services.

Lone parents – the majority of users of family centres – are particularly vulnerable to exclusion from effective citizenship given the pressures they live under – which are especially severe in Britain and the USA. For example, Sorensen (1989) found that while in Western Europe and the USA single mothers are poorer than married couples with children, in the UK 23 per cent of single mothers with one child and 32 per cent of those with two or more children had an income of less than 50 per cent of the median in the country. In comparison, the corresponding figures for married couples were 2 per cent and 13 per cent. In the USA the differences were even larger. Contrast this with the situation in Holland and Sweden, where single mothers are still more likely to be poor than are couples with children, but the differences are substantially smaller. Lone mothers in Britain are at risk of their poverty being compounded by social isolation, which in turn contributes to poor physical and mental health (Popay and Jones, 1990). For many women trapped in this way, the only escape may appear to be dependence on a new man– with implications for their children, who may become vulnerable to new tensions and perhaps abuse. Yet many poor parents might be able to escape welfare dependence and poverty through employment or training. In all EC countries except Denmark and the UK, labour-force participation rates are higher for lone mothers than for other mothers (Moss, 1988: 39). Kiernan and Wicks (1990) found that in the UK:

> Lone parents . . . have small proportions of household heads in the labour market. In 1987, for example, only 27% of lone parents had earnings as their main source of income. The comparative figure for two parent families was 86%. As a consequence, very large proportions of one parent families depend on income support (supplementary benefit). (Kiernan and Wicks, 1990: 28)
>
> 1 in 6 lone parents claimed supplementary benefit in 1961; by 1987 over two thirds had claimed it. Against the trend in other EC countries, the labour force participation rate of female lone parents in Britain has fallen from 48% in 1977 to 39% in 1985. (*ibid*: 33–4)

One answer to the question 'Why do lone parents in Britain not work?' lies in the benefit system's disincentives. Another answer is in the lack of public daycare for children. Dual-worker families in Britain cope mainly through help from relatives: 65 per cent of pre-school children are cared for by grandmothers, husbands or other relatives. Lone mothers may be more likely to be isolated from relatives, to live in areas without good public transport and not to be car owners. The kind of work they do may be at unsocial hours, so that even if public childcare were available, it might not be flexible enough to cater for children in the evenings and at weekends.

In British policy, lone parenthood is seen as a fixed and separate state from other 'normal' families. Yet research shows that it is increasingly, and for around a third of the population, a stage of family life. Ermisch (1989) has shown that the median duration of lone parenthood through divorce is five years, and of lone parenthood through unmarried motherhood three years. He found the remarriage prospects to be better for those with higher education and in employment: an equal opportunities policy and daycare for children would not only help lone mothers to be independent of the state, but would reduce the incidence of lone parenthood. Families are therefore always in a dynamic relation with the state, with changing needs over the life cycle and at periods of transition. As the Commission of the EC report (1989) on family policies noted, member states' policies were relatively slow in adapting to the pace of change in family structures, and to the changing relationship between families and labour markets. Unfortunately, British policy seems not just to be slow but to ignore such changes – or rather, to try to stop them by forcing a return to 'traditional' family forms.

The New Right has used two ideas to promote this: active citizenship and consumerism. The 'active citizen' is the individual who informally provides or buys services in a 'responsible' fashion: this concept is silent on the reciprocal responsibilities of the state and those of social groups in society. Consumer sovereignty and the principles of choice underlay the major Conservative social legislation of the 1980s – in education, housing and local government finance, as well as childcare and community care. The government has claimed that the outcome will be less state intervention as power and choice are devolved to smaller units – schools, self-help groups, etc. This pushing back of the boundaries of care and social provision towards the consumers themselves has been twinned with an attack on the powers and resources of local government. As Glennester *et al.*, (1991) demonstrate:

> if local authorities lose all their significance, there will be nothing to set between small scale semi-representative bodies and a very powerful central state. Poor tenants or school governing bodies, or small voluntary organizations, will be largely powerless in this situation. Local authorities now provide some counter-balance to central power. What we may face is the problem of the excluded middle in the hierarchy of political power. (Glennester *et al.*, 1991: 413)

What is needed, then, in the British context is a strengthening of local government and of its accountability to its voters. User involvement in social services is an important control on professional power, but decisions about what services should be provided (and in what way) should not be left to groups who are relatively powerless themselves, and who are in any case faced with cash-starved local authority and voluntary agency services. If family centres were part of a spectrum of childcare and family support services provided by powerful and generous local authorities, they would have real potential to transform the lives of those they are targeted on. Pluralism 'works' only where the state takes a coordinating role; in the Netherlands, for instance, too much reliance on voluntary provision was found to produce 'lack of coordination, variable and incomplete coverage, and an absence of democratic accountability' (Johnson, 1987: 113). The emphasis on the subsidiarity principle in Germany, however, regulates quality and choice much more effectively, and connects user involvement or self-help with local democratic structures.

The French situation again provides an example of how things might work: strong decentralized government, coordinated and animated by a series of government initiatives developed in partnership with independent organizations, gives an overall sense of direction and of the common good around which local needs are met or planned for. Children are assumed to need services in their own right, as future French citizens, to underpin the education system, and as recognition of the care given in the family. While this attitude may reflect a certain paternalism, it nevertheless means that high-quality services are delivered to families – though there are still significant gaps – and that there is some sharing of the burden between family and state.

Decentralization and social action are certainly familiar to British readers in their encouragment of user involvement, and in their attempt to contain welfare expenditure by stopping the decline of informal care and networks. But there are significant differences. First, in France economic development is connected with social action (urban renewal, job creation and training). While social workers have begun to fear that too much is being asked of them, they are not alone in their reponsibilities. The second difference lies in the powerful local partnerships and committees which promote social action and local development: social work is highly visible and itself valorized by the new emphasis on its role. The third difference is that (despite the recent *rigueur* in public expenditure) families and children have the basic infrastructure of good daycare services and generous benefits: the 'crises' of the family are discussed against a different assumption about citizenship: the good citizen uses society's services, rather than managing without or buying his own in the private sector. Despite the Socialists' backtracking from some of the more 'utopian' ideas of the early 1980s – for instance, in the downplaying of their early policies to promote women's rights in employment and training in favour of family policy with natalist language and traditional images (Reynolds, 1988) – there is a fundamental commitment (expressed, for instance, in National Plans) to lessening strains on family life and to improving the quality of childhood.

So while the French stress – in crime prevention (King, 1988) as much as family policy – state responsibility to promote social cohesion and integration (which has included an expansion of social work and community work), British governments since the mid 1970s have posed welfare intervention and its professionals as exacerbating social problems rooted in lack of self-discipline and selfishness. The French, like the EC policies discussed, have attempted to go with the grain of change, and to work on society and social policies rather than blaming deviant families for producing a crime-prone and welfare dependent underclass.

Conclusion: supporting the family and equal opportunities

If family centres were provided in the context of an expanded range of choice and provision in the public childcare system, they could increase their potential as innovative and creative resources. This could have occurred if the understanding of child abuse had been wider than the focus on intrafamilial abuse. As Gil (1970) noted, we should understand child welfare in much wider terms than its familial and psychological aspects. Racism, poverty, unequal access to good daycare, health care, schools; poor housing and public play facilities: all these inflict deficits upon children's well-being. Policies which sanction this state of inequality in society are abusive.

The consequences for children of British attitudes to family services is that what public daycare remains takes the most deprived and disturbed children. By contrast, professional and middle-class parents may pay for their children to attend private nurseries. There is thus a widening class and ethnic differential between the two types of provision. Most children whose parents work are cared for by relatives: such care is hidden and unregulated, and may range from the best to neglect. Another large proportion of children attend childminders: this is regulated, but of variable quality, and characterized by a high turnover; it is inherently unstable. So too are the day nursery system *and* the private nanny system because the pay, training and status of nursery nurses are low. The childcare system (extending into the residential sector) is unstable, and most unstable for the children who are most in need of good-quality compensatory care, or refuge, care or treatment if they have been abused. Playgroups have been heavily promoted by both the major political parties, but quality is variable, staff have low levels of training, and the hours are not suitable for working mothers. In short, the consequence for children is that the public care system, and its relations in the private, informal and voluntary sectors, is highly variable in quality, and unstable. The Conservative government has concurred with this system by failing to set a national standard, strategy, or target for daycare for children, preferring to leave it as a private matter, or a matter for employers to negotiate with employees. Voluntary organizations are encouraged to join the market, yet are not given the means to provide services of the quality they, or users, would like to see.

Important changes occurred in the British child protection system during the 1980s which will go on developing in the 1990s, such is their momentum. My fear is that (as Nelson [1984] would argue) the focus on children has been used to redraw the lines of conventional and normal family life and of normal male and female roles – especially of male behaviour, in an era of anxiety about the man's place in the family. The state promotes female responsibility: in health and education, as well as in childcare itself. Male and paternal authority is underlined in delinquency policies (fining parents) and in making 'errant' fathers pay maintenance.

The emphasis on child abuse (within the family) has meant that some of the broader functions and possibilities of childcare services – for instance, providing compensatory care and education to prevent the marginalization of groups of children rather than individual children in need – are not addressed at all. There are social benefits to children, but there is also the need to provide good daycare for them so that their mothers can work and reduce their poverty, and improve their morale. Another objective – that of trying to make divisions of labour *within* the family more just – is not even envisaged (hardly surprising, as only Sweden has stated this as an aim of its childcare policies [Melhuish and Moss, 1991]). The family centre approach to childcare means that the opportunity for changing the childcare and family services into something which would support most families in their needs – and that includes changing domestic divisions of labour and promoting more flexible patterns of work – is lost. Instead families are shown images and models of how they should be, and given only limited services to support them in what is essentially a self-help system. The social rights needed for effective citizenship and participation are lacking.

The 1989 Children Act pushes responsibility back on to families, and places a duty on local authorities to provide services, but only to children 'in need'. There is no corresponding duty on central government to fund and support these services, so local authorities will be forced to continue rationing services which will consequently continue to be stigmatized. Family centres will lose their potential genuinely to support and empower families if their services continue to be restricted and if users feel a sense of shame or incompetence.

It may be that British society (as opposed to the state) is damaged by such a limited childcare, youth and family policy. It suffers in the lack of investment in the quality of its population, in health, emotional and educational terms. It suffers in the growing numbers marginalized, excluded and trapped in poverty and dependence (whether on the state or on relatives) who cannot contribute to their community or the common good. Women in particular suffer from the lack of opportunities for access to labour markets or training, and from the reinforcement of their caring tasks without services (let alone choices) to help them. Children suffer from their privatized existences within the family and the lack of opportunities for safe, sociable and creative play in public spaces with professional childcare workers. They suffer from the variable quality of provision and lack of equity in access to services, or in services for the poor which have a central focus on reform of parents rather than promotion of healthy childhood.

So while family centres, in my view, have a potential to support families, they should have a core of good-quality, professional childcare services. They should articulate with labour markets and the training system and provide opportunities for women, both through adult education and counselling within the centres and by providing daycare to enable them to become independent and fulfilled. There should be choice, not simply a child protection or family therapy service which poor families are forced to use for lack of alternatives. Within family centres there should be a range of services and types of user, so that families who are referred because of poor childcare are not isolated, but integrated with healthier and stronger families and groups.

The principle of participation and user involvement is an important one, but one which runs the risk of exploiting users' labour, or of coercing such involvement, if there is not a genuine range of services to choose from, and if the services do not provide the means of making such participation effective. There should be a range of services so that families are not stigmatized: child protection work should be in the context of a range of family support services, activities and methods, and social workers need to view use of day and residential childcare services more positively, not as a sign of failure.

Finally, social work needs a broader remit: crisis work should be only part of general community development; the social action wing of social work should be considered as important as the policing role. Only thus will family centres move out of their narrow association with families who don't cope to become, as some aim to do, general services for families at a neighbourhood level, genuinely sharing care between family and the collectivity, and genuinely offering opportunities to those who use them.

BIBLIOGRAPHY

Abrams, P. (1980) 'Social change, social networks and neighbourhood care', in *Social Work Service*, February.

Adamson, J. and Warren, C. (1983) *Welcome to St Gabriel's!*, London: Children's Society.

Ahmed, S. (1987) 'Racism in child care', in Stone, W. and Warren, C. (eds), *Protection or Prevention: A critical look at the voluntary child care sector*, London: National Council of Voluntary Child Care Organizations.

Anderson, M.(1971) *Family Structure in Nineteenth Century Lancashire*, Cambridge: Cambridge University Press.

Archard, P. (1979) *Vagrancy, Alcoholism and Social Control*, London: Macmillan.

Badinter, E. (1981) *The Myth of Motherhood: An historical view of the maternal instinct*, London: Souvenir Press.

Baher, E. *et al.* (1976) *At Risk: An account of the work of the Battered Child Research Unit*, London: NSPCC.

Baker, J. (1986) 'Comparing national priorities: Family and population policies in France', *Journal of Social Policy* **15** (4).

The Barclay Report (1982) *Social Workers: Their role and tasks*, London: Bedford Square Press/NCVO.

Barker, D. (1978) 'The regulation of marriage: Repressive benevolence', in Littlejohn, G. (ed.) *Power and the State*, London: Croom Helm.

Barritt, G. E. (ed.) (1979) *Family Life*, papers from the 1978 NCH Conference, London: National Children's Home.

Bebbington, A. and Miles, J. (1989) 'Children who enter local authority Care', *British Journal of Social Work* **19** (5).

Becker, H. (1963) *Outsiders – Studies in the sociology of deviance*, New York: Free Press.

Becker, S. and Golding, P. (1991) 'On the breadline', *Community Care*, 17 January.

Behlmer, G. (1982) *Child Abuse and Moral Reform in England 1870–1908*, Stanford, CA: Stanford University Press.

Beresford, P. and Croft, S. (1984) 'Welfare pluralism: The new face of pluralism', *Critical Social Policy* **9**.

Berger, J. (1965) 'Towards a sociological analysis of psychoanalysis', *Social Research* **32** (1).

Bernstein, B. (1971) *Class, Codes and Control*, vol. 1 (see 'A critique of the concept of compensatory education'), London: Routledge & Kegan Paul.

Bernstein, B. (1975) *Class, Codes and Control*, vol. 3, London: Routledge & Kegan Paul.

Birchall, D. (1982) 'Family centres', *Concern* (journal of the National Children's Bureau) **43**.

Blau, P. and Scott, R. (1963) *Formal Organisations: A comparative approach*, London: Routledge & Kegan Paul.

Bowlby, J. (1952): *Maternal Care and Mental Health*, Geneva: WHO.

Brenton, M. (1985) 'Privatisation and the voluntary sector', in Jones, C. and Brenton, M. (eds), *Year Book of Social Policy in Britain 1984–5*, Jones, C. and Brenton, M. (eds), London: Routledge & Kegan Paul.

Brewster, C. and Teague, P. (1989) *European Community Social Policy: Its impact on the UK*, London: IPM.

Brill, J. (1976) 'Langtry Family Centre', in Olsen, M.R. (ed.), *Different Approaches in Social Work with the Mentally Disordered*, Birmingham: British Association of Social Workers.

Brimblecombe, F.S.W. (1976) 'How about parents as partners?', *Social Work Service* **9**.

Bronfenbrenner, U. (1974) 'Children, families and social policy: An American perspective', in DHSS, *The Family in Society: Dimensions of parenthood*, London: HMSO.

Brown, G. and Harris, T. (1978) *Social Origins of Depression*, London: Tavistock.

Burton, F. and Carlen, P. (1979) *Official Discourse*, London: Routledge.

Caisse Nationale d'Allocations Familiales (1987–8) *Le Travail social des Caisses d'Allocations Familiales*, Dossiers CNAF no. 4, Paris: CNAF.

Campbell, B. (1988): *Unofficial Secrets: Child sexual abuse – the Cleveland case*, London: Virago.

Cannan, C. (1990) 'Supporting the family? An assessment of family centres', in Manning, N. and Ungerson, C. (eds), *Social Policy Review 1989–90*, Harlow: Longman.

Cannan, C., Berry, L. and Lyons, K. (1992) *Social Work and Europe*, Basingstoke: NASW/Macmillan.

Cheetham, J. (1981) 'Introduction' to Cheetham, J. *et al.* (eds), *Social Work and Community Work in a Multi-Racial Society*, London: Harper and Row/Open University.

Coffield, F., Robinson, P. and Sarsby, J. (1981) *A Cycle of Deprivation? A case study of four families*, London: Heinemann.

Cohen, B. and Fraser, N. (1991) *Childcare in a Modern Welfare System*, London: Institute for Public Policy Research.

Cohen, S. (1985) *Visions of Social Control: Crime, punishment and classification*, Cambridge: Polity Press.

Collins, M. (1990) 'A guaranteed minimum income in France?', *Social Policy and Administration* **24** (2).

Comfort, A. (1967) *The Anxiety Makers: Some curious preoccupations of the medical profession*, London: Nelson.

Commission of the European Communities (1989) *Communication on Family Policies*, COM89 363, Brussels.

Cooper, C. (1984) 'Alfred White Franklin: Obituary', *BASPCAN News* (British Association for the Study and Prevention of Child Abuse and Neglect), 13 November.

Coote, A., Harman, H. and Hewitt, P. (1990) *The Family Way: A new approach to policy-making*, London: Institute for Public Policy Research.

Coote, N. (1989) 'Catholic social teaching', *Social Policy and Administration* **23** (2).

Corsellis, G. (1977) 'Home-Start, Leicester', *Social Work Service* **14**.

Court, J. (1969) 'Battering parents', *Social Work*, January.

Court, J. (1974) 'Characteristics of parents and children', in Carter, J. (ed.) *The Maltreated Child*, London: Priory Press.

Court Report (1976) *Child Health Services*, London, HMSO.

Craig, G. and Glendinning, C. (1990) 'Parenting in poverty', *Community Care*, 15 March.

Creighton, S.J. (1984) *Trends in Child Abuse*, London: NSPCC.

Croft, S. and Beresford, P. (1989) 'Decentralisation and the personal social services', in Langan, M. and Lee, P. (eds), *Radical Social Work Today*, London: Unwin Hyman.

Croft, S. and Beresford, P. (1990) *From Paternalism to Participation: Involving people in social services*, London: Open Services Project/ Joseph Rowntree Foundation.

Crowe, B. (1983) (4th edn) *The Playgroup Movement*, London: Unwin Paperbacks.

Dale, P. (1984) 'Three act tragedies', *Community Care*, 20 September.

Dale, P., Davies, M., Morrison, T. and Walters, J. (1986) *Dangerous Families*, London: Tavistock.

Dalley, G. (1988) *Ideologies of Caring: Rethinking community and collectivism*, Basingstoke: Macmillan.

David, M. (1985) 'Motherhood and social policy: A matter of education', in *Critical Social Policy* 12.

Davies, C. (1984) 'GPs and the pull of prevention', *Sociology of Health and Illness* 6 (3).

Davin, A. (1978) 'Imperialism and motherhood', *History Workshop Journal* 5.

Dennett, J., James, E., Room, G. and Watson, P. (1982) *Europe Against Poverty: The European Poverty Programme 1975–80*, London: Bedford Square Press.

Dennis, S. and Wallis, S. (1982) *Family Centres and the Day Nursery Service in Lambeth*, London Borough of Lambeth Research Section.

Department of Education and Science (1972) *Education: A framework for expansion*, London: HMSO.

Department of Education and Science (1975) *Educational Disadvantage: Perspectives and policies. Report of a conference*, London: HMSO.

Department of Health (1989) *Caring for People: Community care in the next decade and beyond*, London: HMSO.

Department of Health and Social Security (1971) *Better Services for the Mentally Ill*, London: HMSO.

Department of Health and Social Security (1974) *The Family in Society: Dimensions of parenthood – a report of a seminar*, London: HMSO.

Department of Health and Social Security (1976) *Prevention and Health – Everybody's business*, London: HMSO.

Department of Health and Social Security (1985) *Social Work Decision-Making in Child Care*, London: HMSO.

Department of Health and Social Security/Department of Education and Science (1976) *Low Cost Day Provision for the Under Fives – papers from a conference*, London: HMSO.

Department of Social Security (1990) *Children Come First: The government's proposals on the maintenance of children*, London: HMSO.

Dingwall, R. and Eekelaar, J. (1984) 'Rethinking child protection', in Freeman, M. (ed.), *The State, the Law and the Family*, London: Tavistock.

Dingwall, R., Eekelaar, J. and Murray, T. (1983) *The Protection of Children – State intervention and family life*, Oxford: Blackwell.

Dominelli, L. (1986) 'Father–daughter incest: Patriarchy's shameful secret', *Critical Social Policy* 12.

Donzelot, J. (1980) *Policing the Family: Welfare versus the state*, London: Hutchinson.

Edwards, S. (1984) *Women on Trial*, Manchester: Manchester University Press.

Edwards, S. (1989) *Policing 'Domestic' Violence: Women, the law and the state*, London: Sage.

Ehrenreich, B. and English, D. (1976) *For Her Own Good: 150 years of the experts' advice to women*, London: Pluto Press.

Ely, D. (1984) *Family Centre Evaluation*, part of an unpublished MSc. dissertation, University of Surrey.

Ely, P. and Stanley, C. (1990): *Delinquency Prevention and Child Protection in France*, London: NACRO.

Ennew, J. (1986) *The Sexual Exploitation of Children*, Cambridge: Polity Press.

Ermisch, J. (1989) 'Divorce: Economic antecedents and aftermath', in Joshi, H. (ed.) *The Changing Population of Britain*, Oxford: Blackwell.

Fells, J.R. and de Gruchy, S. (1991) 'Explaining the "need" for family centres: The perceptions of social workers and their importance for planning', *British Journal of Social Work* **21** (2).

Ferri, E. and Niblett, R. (1977) *Disadvantaged Families and Playgroups*, London: NFER.

Ferri, E., Birchall, D., Gingell, V. and Gipps, C. (1981) *Combined Nursery Centres: A new approach to education and daycare*, London: National Children's Bureau/Macmillan.

Finch, J. (1984) 'The deceit of self-help', in *Journal of Social Policy* **13** (1).

Finch, J. (1989) 'Social policy, social engineering and the family in the 1990s', in Bulmer, M., Lewis, J. and Piachaud, D. (eds), *The Goals of Social Policy*, London: Unwin Hyman.

Fitzgerald, T. (1983) 'The New Right and the family', in Loney, M. *et al.* (eds), *Social Policy and Social Welfare*, Milton Keynes: Open University Press.

Foucault, M. (1976) *The Birth of the Clinic*, London: Tavistock.

Freeman, M.D.A. (1983) *The Rights and Wrongs of Children*, London: Frances Pinter.

Freidson, E. (1970) *Profession of Medicine*, New York: Dodd Mead & Co.

Freire, P. (1970) *Pedagogy of the Oppressed*, Harmondsworth: Penguin.

Frost, N. and Stein, M. (1989) *The Politics of Child Welfare: Inequality, power and change*, Hemel Hempstead: Harvester Wheatsheaf.

Garrish, S. (1986) *Centralisation and Decentralisation in England and France*, School of Advanced Urban Studies, University of Bristol.

Geach, H. and Szwed, E. (1983) *Providing Civil Justice for Children*, London: Arnold.

Gelles, R.J. (1979) 'Child abuse and psychopathology: A sociological critique and reformulation' and 'The social construction of child abuse', in Gil, D. (ed.), *Child Abuse and Violence*, New York: Ams Press.

Gibbons, J. (1990) *Family Support and Prevention: Studies in local areas*, London: National Institute for Social Work/HMSO.

Gil, D. (1970) *Violence Against Children*, Cambridge, MA: Harvard University Press.

Gil, D. (ed.) (1979) *Child Abuse and Violence*, New York: Ams Press.

Glennester, H., Power, A. and Travers, T. (1991) 'A New Enlightenment or a New Leviathan', *Journal of Social Policy* **20** (3).

Goldstein, J., Freud, A. and Solnit A.J. (1973) *Beyond the Best Interests of the Child*, New York: Free Press.

Gordon, L. (1988) *Heroes of their Own Lives*, London: Viking Penguin.

Gouldner, A.F. (1973) *For Sociology*, Harmondsworth: Penguin.

Graham, H. (1979) 'Prevention and health: Every mother's business – a comment on child health policies in the 1970s', in Harris, C. (ed.), *The Sociology of the Family: New directions for Britain*, Sociological Review Monograph, University of Keele.

Hadley, R., Dale, S. and Sills, P. (1984) *Decentralising Social Services: A model for change*, London: Bedford Square Press.

Hall, P. (1976) *Reforming the Welfare: The politics of change in the personal social services*, London: Heinemann.

Halmos, P. (1967) 'The personal service society', *British Journal of Sociology* **18**.

Halsey, A. (ed.) (1972) *Educational Priority: Problems and policies*, London: HMSO.

Hanmer, J. and Statham, D. (1988) *Women and Social Work: Towards a woman-centred practice*, Basingstoke: Macmillan/BASW.

Hardyment, C. (1983) *Dream Babies: Childcare from Locke to Spock*, London: Cape.

Harrison, M. (1981) 'Home-Start', *Early Childhood*, February.

Hasler, J. (1984) *Family Centres: Different expressions: same principles*, London: Children's Society.

Hatch, S. and Hadley, R. (1981) *Social Welfare and the Failure of the State: Centralised social services and participatory alternatives*, London: Allen and Unwin.

Hegar, R.L. (1989) 'The rights and status of children: International concerns for social work', *International Social Work* **32**.

Heidensohn, F. (1985) *Women and Crime*, London: Macmillan.

Heiser, B. and Godfrey, M. (1984) *Under-Fives in Camden: The parents' views*, unpublished report from the London Borough of Camden, Chief Executive/Social Services Department.

Henriques, U.R.Q. (1979) *Before the Welfare State*, Harlow: Longman.

HMSO (1991) *The Citizen's Charter: Raising the Standard* (Conservatives' Charter), London: HMSO.

Hoghughi, M. (1991) 'Punishing parents for the children's sins', *The Magistrate*, March.

Holman, R. (1976) *Inequality in Child Care*, London: CPAG.

Holman, R. (1978) *Poverty*, London: Martin Robertson.

Holman, R. (1983) *Resourceful Friends: Skills in community work*, London: Children's Society.

Holman, R. (1985) 'Helping or hoaxing the poor?', *New Society*, 18 April.
Holman, R. (1986) 'Under-fives running out of time', *The Guardian*, 25 June.
Holman, R. (1988) *Putting Families First: Prevention and child care: a study of prevention by statutory and voluntary agencies*, Basingstoke: Macmillan.
Home Office (1948) *Circular on the Children Act* to local authorities.
Home Office (1965) *The Child, the Family and the Young Offender*, London: HMSO.
Home Office (1980) *Young Offenders*, London: HMSO.
Home Office (1990) *Crime, Justice and Protecting the Public*, London: HMSO
Home Office/DHSS (1979) *Marriage Matters*, London: HMSO.
Humphries, J. (1981) 'Protective legislation, the capitalist state and working class men: The case of the 1842 Mines Regulation Act', *Feminist Review* 7.
Illsey, R. (1981) 'Problems of dependency groups: The care of the elderly, the handicapped and the chronically ill', *Social Science and Medicine* **15a**.
Ingleby Report (1960) *Report of the Committee on Children and Young Persons*, London: HMSO.
Jackson, S. (1983) *The Education of the Child in Care*, University of Bristol.
Jeffreys, S. (1985) *The Spinster and her Enemies: Feminism and sexuality 1880–1930*, London: Pandora.
Johnson, M. (1972) *Professions and Power*, London: Macmillan.
Johnson, N. (1987) *The Welfare State in Transition: The theory and practice of welfare pluralism*, Hemel Hempstead: Harvester Wheatsheaf.
Jones, M. (1968) *Social Psychiatry in Practice*, Harmondsworth: Penguin.
Jordan, W. (1981) 'Family therapy – An outsider's view', *Journal of Family Therapy*, **3**.
Jordan, W. (1987/8) 'Why is prevention neglected?', *Family Rights Group Bulletin*.
Joseph, A. and Parfit, J. (1972) *Playgroups in an Area of Social Need*, London: NFER.
Joseph, Sir K. (1972a) 'The cycle of deprivation', speech to the Pre-School Playgroups Association Conference, 29 June in Butterworth, E. and Holman, R. (1975) *Social Welfare in Modern Britain*, London: Fontana.
Joseph, Sir K. (1972b): 'The parental role', speech to the National Children's Bureau Conference, in *Concern*, Winter 1972–3.
Joseph, Sir K. (1974) 'Foreword' to Kellmer Pringle, *The Needs of Children*.
Kellmer Pringle, M. (1974) *The Needs of Children: A personal perspective prepared for the DHSS*, London: Hutchinson.

Kempe, C.H. *et al.* (1962) 'The battered child syndrome', *Journal of the American Medical Association* **181** (1).

Kempe, R.S. and Kempe, C.H. (1978) *Child Abuse*, London: Fontana.

Kerslake, A. and Cramp, J. (1988) *A New Child Care Model: The evidence for change*, Bath Social Policy Papers, University of Bath.

Kiernan, K. and Wicks, M. (1990) *Family Change and Future Policy*, London: Family Policy Studies Centre.

King, M. (1988) *How to Make Social Crime Prevention Work: the French experience*, London: NACRO.

King, R., Raynes, N. and Tizard, J. (1975) *Patterns of Residential Care*, London: Routledge & Kegan Paul.

Labour Party (1991) *Citizen's Britain: Labour's better deal for consumers and citizens*, London: Labour Party.

Laing, R.D. and Esterson, A. (1964) *Sanity, Madness and the Family*, London: Tavistock.

Land, H. (1979) 'The boundaries between the state and the family', in Harris, C. (ed.), *The Sociology of the Family: New directions for Britain*, Sociological Review Monograph, University of Keele.

Land, H. (1989) 'The construction of dependency', in Bulmer, M. *et al.* (eds), *The Goals of Social Policy*, London: Unwin Hyman.

Lasch, C. (1979) *The Culture of Narcissism*, New York: Abacus.

Leprince, F. (1991) 'Day care for young children in France', in Melhuish, E.C. and Moss, P. (eds) (1991) *Daycare for young children: International perspectives*, London: Routledge.

Lewis, J. (1980) *The Politics of Motherhood: Child and maternal welfare in England 1900–1939*, London: Croom Helm.

Lewis, J. (1989) 'Social policy and the family – Introduction', in Bulmer, M. *et al.* (eds), *The Goals of Social Policy*, London: Unwin Hyman.

Liffman, M. (1978) *Power for the Poor: The Family Centre Project*, Sydney: Allen & Unwin.

Linthwaite, P. (1982) *Eliza Street Family Day Centre: A descriptive evaluation*, Save the Children Fund: unpublished.

Lister, R. (1990) *The Exclusive Society: Citizenship and the Poor*, London: CPAG.

London Borough of Brent (1985) *A Child in Trust: The report of the inquiry into the circumstances surrounding the death of Jasmine Beckford*.

Longford Report (1964) *Crime: A challenge to us all*, London: Labour Party Study Group.

Luckock, B. (1986) 'An opportunity model of social work practice with children and families', in *Young Family Day Care Newsletter* **17**, May.

McIntosh, M. (1978) 'The state and the oppression of women', in Kuhn, A. and Wolpe, A. (eds), *Feminism and Materialism*, London: Routledge & Kegan Paul.

McIntosh, M. (1984) 'The family, regulation and the public sphere', in

McLellan, G. (ed.), *The State and Society in Contemporary Britain*, Cambridge: Polity Press.

Mackay, Lord (1989) 'Perceptions of the Children Bill and beyond', *New Law Journal*, 14 April.

Madge, N. (ed.) (1983) *Families at Risk*, SSRC/DHSS Studies in Deprivation and Disadvantage, London: Heinemann.

Marshall, T. (1982) 'Infant care: A day nursery under the microscope', in *Social Work Service* **32**.

Mayer, J. and Timms, N. (1970) *The Client Speaks*, London: Routledge & Kegan Paul.

Melhuish, E.C. and Moss, P. (eds) (1991) *Daycare for Young Children: International perspectives*, London: Routledge.

Meny, Y. (1987) 'The socialist decentralisation', in Ross, G. *et al.* (eds): *The Mitterrand Experiment: Continuity and change in modern France*, Cambridge: Polity Press.

Meyer, P. (1983) *The Child and the State: The intervention of the state in family life*, Cambridge: Cambridge University Press.

Milham, S., Bullock, R. and Cherrett, P. (1975) 'A conceptual scheme for the comparative analysis of residential institutions', in Tizard, J. (ed.), *Varieties of Residential Experience*, London: Routledge & Kegan Paul.

Morgan, D. (1985) *The Family, Politics and Social Theory*, London: Routledge & Kegan Paul.

Moss, P. (1988) *Childcare and Equality of Opportunity: Consolidated report to the European Commission*, Commission of the EC, Brussels.

Moss, P. (1991) 'Daycare in the UK', in Melhuish, E.C. and Moss, P. (eds) (1991) *Daycare for Young Children: International perspectives*, London: Routledge.

Mount, F. (1982) *The Subversive Family: An alternative history of love and marriage*, London: Jonathan Cape.

Murray, C. (1984) *Losing Ground: American social policy 1950–1980*, New York: Basic Books.

Nelson, B. (1984) *Making an Issue of Child Abuse: Political agenda setting and social problems*, Chicago: University of Chicago Press.

Oliver, M. (1990) *The Politics of Disablement*, Basingstoke: Macmillan.

Packman, J. (1981) *The Child's Generation*, London: Allen & Unwin.

Packman, J. and Jordan, B. (1991) 'The Children Act: Looking forward, looking back', *British Journal of Social Work* **21**: (4).

Packman, J., Randall, J. and Jacques, N. (1986) *Who Needs Care? Social work decisions about children*, Oxford: Blackwell.

Parker, H. and Giller, H. (1981) 'More and less the same: British delinquency research since the sixties', *British Journal of Criminology* **21** (3).

Parker, R. (ed.) (1980) *Caring for Separated Children: Plans, procedures and priorities*, London: Macmillan.

Parton, N. (1985) *The Politics of Child Abuse*, London: Macmillan.

Pearse, I. and Crocker, L. (1943) *The Peckham Experiment: A study in the living structure of society*, London: George Allen & Unwin.

Pearson, G. (1974) 'Prisons of love: The reification of the family in family therapy', in Armistead, N. (ed.) *Reconstructing Social Psychology*, Harmondsworth: Penguin.

Pelton, L.H. (1978) 'Child abuse and the myth of classlessness', in *American Journal of Orthopsychiatry* **48**.

Perelberg, R.J. and Miller, A.C. (1990) *Gender and Power in Families*, London: Tavistock.

Pfohl, S. (1977) 'The "discovery" of child abuse', *Social Problems* **24** (3).

Phelan, J. (1983) *Family Centres: A study*, London: Children's Society.

Pinchbeck, I. and Hewitt, M. (1973) *Children in English Society*, vol. 2, London: Routledge.

Pitts, J. (1988) *The Politics of Juvenile Crime*, London: Sage.

Platt, A. (1977) *The Child Savers: The invention of delinquency*, Chicago: University of Chicago Press.

Plowden Report (1967) *Children and Their Primary Schools*, Report of the Central Advisory Council for Education, London: HMSO.

Popay, J. and Jones, G. (1990) 'Patterns of health and illness amongst lone parents', in *Journal of Social Policy* **19** (4).

Poster, M. (1978) *Critical Theory of the Family*, London: Pluto Press.

Poulton, G. and James, T. (1975) *Pre-School Learning in the Community*, London: Routledge & Kegan Paul.

Pugh, G. (ed.) (1980) *Preparation for Parenthood: Some current initiatives*, London: National Children's Bureau.

Raymond, J. (1986) 'I am the world', *New Statesman*, 30 May.

Reynolds, S. (1988) 'The French Ministry of Women's Rights 1981–6: Modernisation or marginalisation?', in Gaffney, J. (ed.) *France and Modernisation*, London: Gower.

Riley, D. (1983) *War in the Nursery: Theories of child and mother*, London: Virago.

Robinson, D. (1979): *Talking out of Alcoholism: The self-help process of Alcoholics Anonymous*, London: Croom Helm.

Room, G. *et al.* (1989) 'New poverty in the EC', *Policy and Politics* **17** (2).

Rose, N. (1973) *Ten Therapeutic Playgroups*, London: NSPCC.

Rowe, J. and Lambert, L. (1973) *Children Who Wait*, London: Association of British Adoption Agencies.

Russell Report (1973) *Adult Education: A plan for development*, Department of Education and Science, London: HMSO.

Rutter, M. (1974) 'Dimensions of parenthood: Some myths and suggestions', in DHSS, *The Family in Society: Dimensions of parenthood*, London: HMSO.

Rutter, M. and Madge, N. (1976) *Cycles of Disadvantage*, London: Heinemann.

Rutter, M. and Madge, N. (1976) *Cycles of Disadvantage*, London: Heinemann.

Rutter, M., Quinton, D. and Liddle, C. (1983) 'Parenting in two generations: Looking backwards and looking forwards', in Madge, N. (ed.), *Families at Risk*, London: Heinemann.

Satyamurti, C. (1981) *Occupational Survival: The case of the local authority social worker*, Oxford: Blackwell.

Scull, A. (1984) *Decarceration: Community treatment and the deviant: a radical view*, Cambridge: Polity Press.

Sedgwick, P. (1982) *Psychopolitics*, London: Pluto Press.

The Seebohm Report (1968) *The Report of the Committee on Local Authority and Allied Personal Social Services*, London: HMSO.

Shearer, A. (1981) *Disability: Whose handicap?*, Oxford: Blackwell.

Sheppard, M. (1982) *Perceptions of Child Abuse: A critique of individualism*, University of East Anglia Monograph.

The Short Report (1984) *Report of the House of Commons Select Committee on Children in Care*, London: HMSO.

Skinner, A. and Castle, R. (1969) *78 Battered Children: A Retrospective Study*, London: NSPCC.

Sone, K. (1991) 'Nuclear power?', *Community Care*, 24 January.

Sorensen, A. (1989) 'Women's economic vulnerability: The case of single mothers', paper given at the EC conference on *Poverty Marginalisation and Social Exclusion*', Alghero, April.

Spicker, P. (1991) 'Solidarity', in Room, G. (ed.), *Towards a European Welfare State*, University of Bristol.

Stones, C. (1989) 'Groups and groupings in a family centre', in Brown, A. and Clough, R. (eds), *Groups and Groupings: Life and work in day and residential centres*, London: Tavistock/Routledge.

Strong, P. (1979) *The Ceremonial Order of the Clinic*, London: Routledge & Kegan Paul.

Szasz, T. (1970) 'The myth of mental illness', in *Ideology and Insanity*, Harmondsworth: Penguin.

Thamesdown Voluntary Services Centre (n.d.) *Local Partnership in Action: A look at family projects in Swindon*.

Thayer, P. (1973) 'The Pre-School Playgroups Association and the social services', in *Social Work Service 1*.

Thévenet, A. and Desigaux, J. (1985) *Les Travailleurs Sociaux*, Paris: Presses Universitaires de France.

Thomas, D. (1983) *The Making of Community Work*, London: George Allen & Unwin.

Titmuss, R. (1970) *The Gift Relationship*, London: Allen & Unwin.

Tizard, J., Sinclair, I. and Clarke, R. (1975) *Varieties of Residential Experience*, London: Routledge & Kegan Paul.

Townsend, P. (1974) 'The cycle of deprivation', speech to the British Association of Social Workers, Birmingham.

Townsend, P. (1979) *Poverty in the United Kingdom*, Harmondsworth: Penguin.

Townsend, P. (1990) 'And the walls came tumbling down', *Poverty* (Child Poverty Action Group) **75**.

Treacher, A. and Carpenter, J. (1984) *Using Family Therapy*, Oxford: Blackwell.

Tunnard, J. (1987) 'A decade of the Family Rights Group', in Stone, W. (ed.) *Family Projects*, London: Children's Society.

Tunstill, J. (1985) 'Aiming to prevent misunderstanding', *Social Work Today*, 17 June.

Tunstill, J. (1991) 'Not yet a bed of roses', *Community Care*, 26 September.

Tutt, N. (1981) 'A decade of policy', *British Journal of Criminology* **21** (3).

Urwin, K. (1974) 'Social services – The problems of resources', in Carter, J. (ed.), *The Maltreated Child*, London: Priory Press.

Vandamme, J. (1985) *New Dimensions in European Social Policy*, London: Croom Helm.

van der Eyken, W. (1982) *Home-Start – A four year evaluation*, Leicester: Home-Start Consultancy.

Wadsworth, M. (1979) *The Roots of Delinquency: Infancy, adolescence and crime*, Oxford: Martin Robertson.

Wagner, G. (1979) *Barnardo*, London: Weidenfeld & Nicolson.

Wagner, G. (1982) *Children of the Empire*, London: Weidenfeld and Nicolson.

The Wagner Report (1988) vol. 1: *Residential Care: A Positive Choice*; vol. 2: *The Research Reviewed*, London: National Institute for Social Work.

Walker, H. (1991) 'Family centres', in Carter, P., Jeffs, T. and Smith, M. (eds), *Social Work and Social Welfare Yearbook*, Milton Keynes: Open University Press.

Walrond-Skynner, S. (1979) 'Introduction' to Walrond-Skynner (ed.) *Family and Marital Therapy: A critical approach*, London: Routledge & Kegan Paul.

Walters, M. (1990) 'A feminist perspective in family therapy', in Perelberg, R.J. and Miller, A.C. (eds), *Gender and Power in Families*, London: Tavistock/Routledge.

The Warnock Report (1978) *Report of the Enquiry into the Education of Handicapped Children and Young People: Special educational needs*, London: HMSO.

Warren, C. (1990) *The Potential for Parent Advocacy in Family Centres*, unpublished MPhil thesis, University of Southampton.

Weeks, J. (1981) *Sex, Politics and Society: The regulation of sexuality since 1800*, London: Longman.

West, D.J. (1982) *Delinquency, its Roots, Careers and Prospects*, London: Heinemann.

West, D.J. and Farrington, D. (1971) *Present Conduct and Future Delinquency*, London: Heinemann.

West, D. J. and Farrington, D. (1973) *Who Becomes Delinquent?* London: Heinemann.

Whitfield, R. (1979) 'Education for family responsibility', in Barritt, G.E. (ed.), *Family Life*, papers from the 1978 NCH Conference, London: National Children's Home.

Whitfield, R. (1990) Message from the chairman of the National Family Trust at the XVI International Congress for the Family, Brighton.

Whittaker, J.K. and Garbarino, J. (eds) (1983) *Social Support Networks: Informal helping in the human services*, New York: Aldine.

Whittaker, J., Schinke, S. and Gilchrist, L. (1986) 'The ecological paradigm in child, youth and family services: Implications for policy and practice', *Social Service Review*, Chicago.

Willmott, P. and Mayne, S. (1983) *Families at the Centre: A study of seven action projects*, London: Bedford Square Press/NCVO.

Wilson, H. (1980) 'Parental supervision: A neglected aspect of delinquency', *British Journal of Criminology*, 3 (20).

Wilson, H. and Herbert, G. (1978) *Parents and Children in the Inner City*, London: Routledge & Kegan Paul.

Winnicott, D.W. (1964) *The Child, the Family and the Outside World*, Harmondsworth: Penguin.

The Wolfenden Report (1978) *The Report of the Committee on Voluntary Organisations*, London: Croom Helm.

Woodroofe, K. (1963) *From Charity to Social Work in England and the United States*, London: Routledge & Kegan Paul.

Wootton, A.J. (1977) 'Sharing: Some notes on the organisation of talk in a therapeutic community', *Sociology* **11.**

Zawada, A. (1981) 'An outline of the history and current state of family therapy', in Box, S. *et al.* (eds), *Psychotherapy with Families: An analytical approach*, London: Routledge & Kegan Paul.

INDEX